IN MEMORY
OF THE MICHELIN EMPLOYEES
AND WORKMEN WHO DIED GLORIOUSLY
FOR THEIR COUNTRY

THE BATTLE OF VERDUN

(1914-1918)

VERDUN BURNING IN 1916 DURING BOMBARDMENT WITH INCENDIARY SHELLS.

VERDUN

ORIGIN AND POLITICAL HISTORY

Verdun, one of France's most ancient cities, was first a Gallic, then under the name of "Virodunum Castrum," a Roman fortress. In 843 the celebrated treaty which divided the Carolingian Empire and annexed Verdun to the Kingdom of Lorraine was signed there. From 870 to 879 Verdun became part of France, but in 923 it was incorporated in the German Empire. As a county, it was governed under the feudal system by the hereditary counts, the last of whom was Godefroy de Bouillon, and later by the episcopal counts and bishops.

In the 10th century, Bishop Haimont, of Verdun, persuaded the Count of Verdun to transfer his rights to him. The arrangement was confirmed by Emperor Othon III., but the count's heirs disputed the bishops' title to the town. Later, the burgesses revolted against the authority of the bishops, and after a sanguinary struggle succeeded in throwing off their yoke about the middle of the 13th century. After a long occupation by the Germans, Henri II., King of France, retook Verdun in 1552 and granted it privileges which were confirmed by François II. in 1559. During the Religious Wars, the town was for the Leaguers, and only agreed to receive Henry IV.'s envoy, after that prince's conversion to the Roman Faith. The burgesses did not take the oath of allegiance to the King of France until 1601.

CHIEF MILITARY EVENTS

Both in respect of its geographical position and history, Verdun is a typical fortified town. From time immemorial it has played an important part in resisting invasion, as witness its fortified camp and citadel. Since 1870 it has been the centre of an essential position formed by a rough hemi-cycle of hills and slopes bristling with defensive works and batteries.

Since the year 450, when Attila left it "like a field ravaged by wild beasts," it has been besieged at least ten times.

Charles Quint besieged and took it in 1544, but after a seven years' occupation it was retaken by Henry II. of France in 1552. The Huguenots tried to take it by surprise in 1589, but were unable to overcome the resistance of the burgesses.

Siege of 1792.—In 1792, the Prussians attacked and bombarded the town, defended by Beaurepaire with only thirty-two guns and forty-four artillerymen. The Council of Defence, urged thereto by the Anti-Republican section of the population, decided to capitulate, in spite of opposition on the part of Beaurepaire, who died suddenly soon afterwards at the Town Hall by his own hand, according to some, others holding that he was assassinated. The Prussians occupied the town for six weeks, after the garrison had left. Although it is true that a few women went to the Camp of Bras with an offering of sweetmeats for the King of Prussia, it has not been established that the latter gave a ball at Regret, at which the women of Verdun danced. The victory of Valmy forced the Prussians to leave Verdun. On October 13th Kellermann took possession of the Citadel, and on the 14th the troops of the Republic entered the town. Several of the visitors to the Camp of Bras expiated their regrettable act on the scaffold.

Siege of 1870.—In 1870, Verdun offered a more stubborn resistance. When the Saxon troops, about 10,000 in number, appeared to the east of the town, the garrison of the latter comprised only 1,500 regular troops, including fifty artillerymen, 2,000 "mobiles" (newly levied men) and 1,400 men of the National Sedentary Guard, while its armament consisted of twenty mortars, two howitzers and ninety-six guns, of which only forty-six were rifled. Under the command of General Guérin de Waldersbach, seconded by General Marmier, this small garrison repulsed an attack on August 24th, and refused to surrender. After being reinforced by 2,600 men who had escaped from Sedan, several sallies were made. By September 23rd the enemy had completely encircled the town, and were forcing the inhabitants of the surrounding villages to help with the siege-works. On the night of October 19th thirty sappers, twenty-five artillerymen and 100 foot soldiers surprised the two German batteries on Heyvaux Hill, between Thierville and Regret, on the left bank, and after hand-to-hand fighting, spiked all the guns.

After the fall of Metz, Verdun, besieged by 15,000 men with 140 heavy guns, in addition to field artillery, surrendered on November 8th with the honours of war.

The town had been bombarded three times. On August 24th it received about 2,000 shells; on September 26th the Citadel received 1,000 to 1,200 shells in five hours; on October 13th, 14th and 15th 20,000 to 25,000 shells fell in the town, severely damaging the upper part and the Citadel.

The name of the German Prefect who governed Verdun and the Meuse province was Von Bethmann Hollweg.

Abbreviations: Q.G., *General Headquarters;* P.C., *Post of Commandment.*

German army corps are indicated by Roman figures followed by the letters "C" for the *active* and "R.C." for the *reserve.*

French army corps are indicated by arabic figures followed by the letters "C.A."

German infantry divisions are indicated by their number followed by the letters "D" for the *active,* "R.D." for the *reserve,* "D.L." for the "*Landwehr,*" and "E.D." for the "*Ersatz.*"

French infantry divisions are indicated by their number followed by the letters "D.I."

Verdun played an essential part in the great war.

In 1914, during the battle of the Marne, the army under General Sarrail, resting on Verdun, formed the pivot for Marshal Joffre's manœuvre (*see the Michelin Guide:* **"The Battle of the Marne,"** part III., "*The Revigny Pass*").

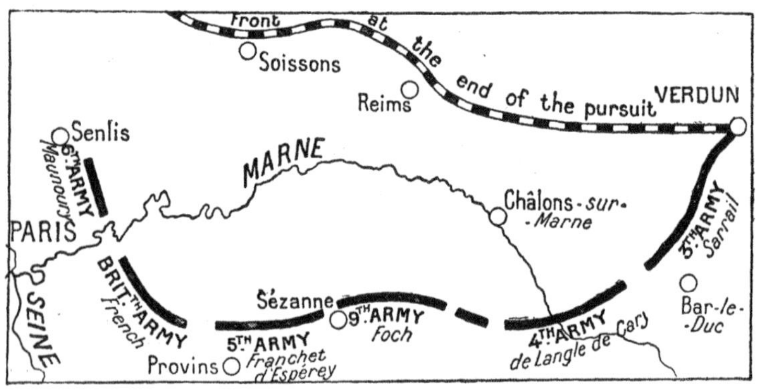

VERDUN—PIVOT OF THE BATTLE OF THE MARNE.

After the battle of the Marne, the Crown Prince established his positions of resistance north of the fortress, on the line Malancourt—Brabant—Haumont—Maucourt. On September 15th, General Sarrail slipped in from this side the 6th C.A. and 72nd R.D., which were sent beyond the advance forts. The enemy sought to isolate and approach Verdun at the same time. The combats which occurred successively on the initiative of each side were indecisive on the north, but not on the S.E.

On September 20th the IIIrd Bavarian Corps attacked the 75th R.D. at Vigneuilles-les-Hatton châtel, and after forcing it to retreat, reached the Meuse Heights. The 6th Corps was hastily transferred to this region, where it checked the German advance. Further to the right, at St. Mihiel, the enemy succeeded on the 25th in forcing the passage of the Meuse and occupied Chauvoncourt.

During October, November and December, the adversaries harassed one another without intermission. In the vicinity of St. Mihiel the enemy maintained their positions on the left bank of the river.

So far from besieging Verdun, as the *Wolff News Agency* falsely announced, or entering it, as a postcard circulated throughout Germany, entitled "*Combats in the streets of Verdun,*" tried to make believe, the Crown Prince was held in check on the general line Vauquois—Malancourt—Brabant—Bois des Caures—Ornes—Fromezey—Hennemont—Combres—Lamorville—Spada—Chauvoncourt. These positions were but slightly modified up to the time of the big attack in February, 1916.

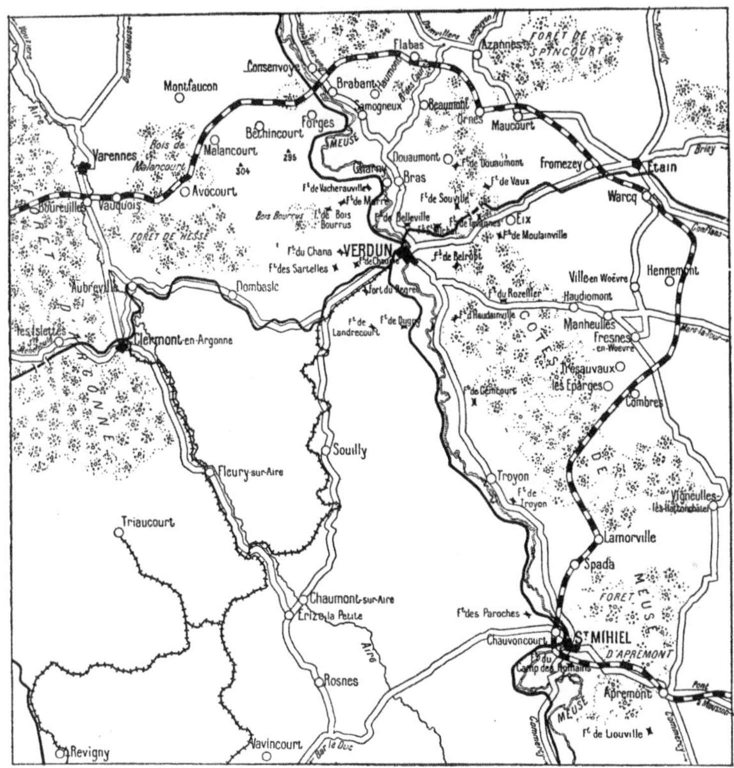

THE VERDUN FRONT, FROM THE BATTLE OF THE MARNE UNTIL THE GREAT GERMAN OFFENSIVE IN 1916.

In February, 1915, the city was bombed by aeroplanes, while the forts of Douaumont and Vaux were shelled by heavy artillery, including 17-inch guns. The Eparges crest, stubbornly held by the enemy since September, 1914, was definitely taken on April 6th by the 12th D.I. after more than a month of the fiercest fighting. This brilliant action was followed by violent counter-attacks by the Vth German corps, the combats being particularly furious on April 24th and May 5th, after which the fighting was less desperate.

On November 25th–26th the enemy attacked to the N.W. of the city, but despite the liberal use of poison gas, they failed to reach the French lines.

Further attacks by the Germans against Forges on January 12th and at Caures Wood on February 12th, 1916, were unsuccessful.

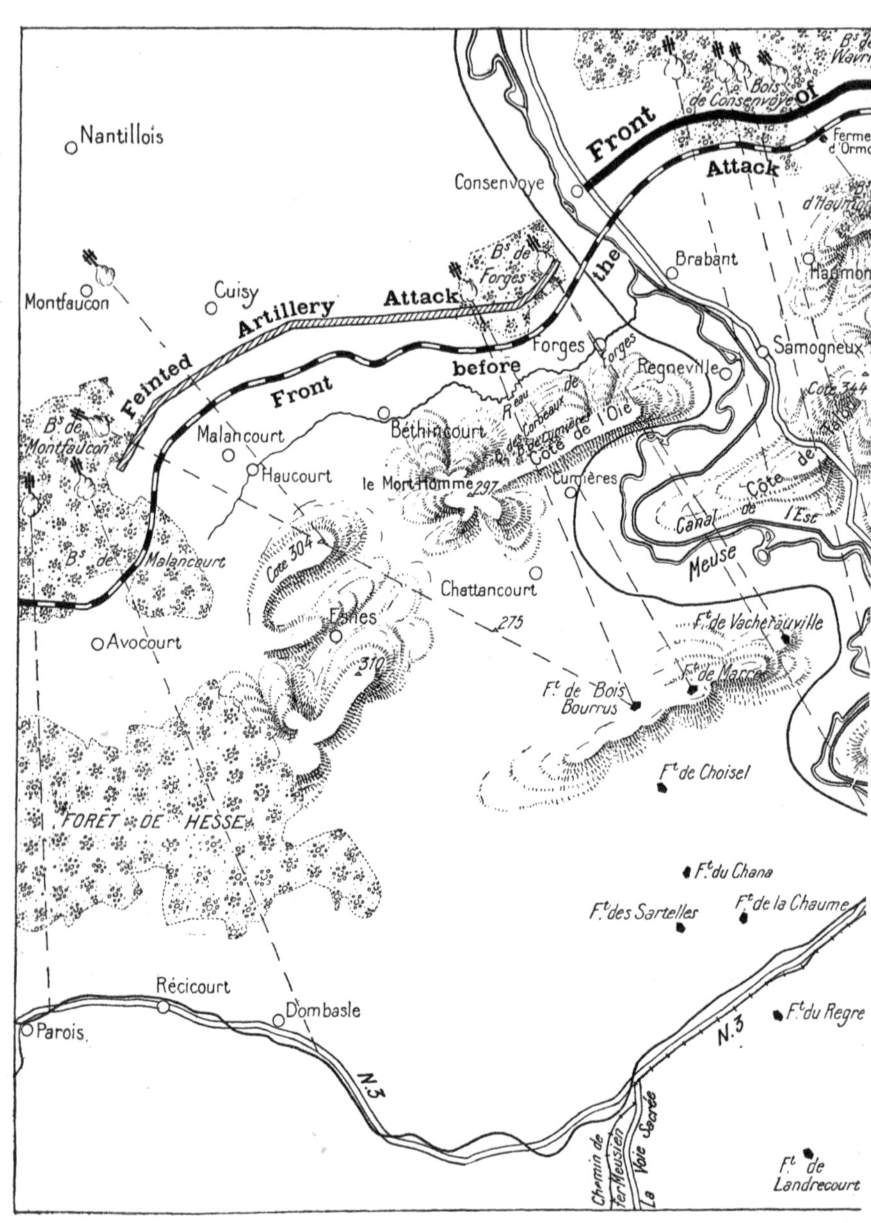

PLAN OF THE GERMA

"Concentrate an all-powerful artillery, cut with gun-fire the or defences, isolating their occupants with heavy artillery barrag crushing the last vestiges of resistance,"—such was the "kolossa

FENSIVE OF FEBRUARY, 1916.

in railway connecting Verdun with France, crush the French
n rush the town with huge masses of men, irrespective of losses,
n which the Germans set out to execute on February 21st, 1916.

THE BATTLE OF VERDUN

A battle which was destined to last much longer than the entire Franco-German war of 1870-1871, and which absorbed the efforts of Germany throughout the year, began on February 21st, 1916.

The choice of this battlefield was perhaps less paradoxical than has been said. For the German High Command to take Verdun was to crush the French right, capture an important strategical position and secure an immense moral effect. Moreover, the enemy feared an Allied offensive and was disturbed by the continued increase of their strength in men and material. To forestall this offensive was to make it fail and keep the initiative of the operations. Moreover, the Germans desired to impress the public opinion of the world, which had begun to doubt their ultimate victory. Greece and Roumania seemed inclined to abandon their neutrality, and the time appeared ripe to prove by a crushing blow that German force had not diminished. Lastly, they were influenced by home political considerations; the rationing of the population had depressed the public *morale* and provoked dissension between the political parties and the states; the prestige of the Crown Prince, after his failure in the Argonne, had considerably declined; a great victory was necessary to strengthen German *morale*, appease dissension and, by rehabilitating the Crown Prince, enhance the prestige of the Imperial family.

The Germans, who had fourteen railways at their disposal, and who, during a long and careful preparation, had concentrated seven army corps and extraordinarily powerful artillery, comprising at least 3,000 guns of all calibres, attacked the French, who had a river in their rear and whose one solitary broad-gauge railway was under enemy gun-fire. By sacrificing men and material on a lavish scale the enemy counted on rapidly overcoming all obstacles, level the French trenches, crush the centres of resistance under a deluge of 17-inch, 15-inch and 12-inch shells, isolate them with barrage fire from

GENERALS JOFFRE AND PÉTAIN AT THE G.H.Q. OF THE 2ND FRENCH ARMY AT SOUILLY, IN FEBRUARY, 1916.

8-inch guns and poison-gas shells, and occupy the destroyed positions—such were to be the German tactics. They were so sure, by repeated smashing blows, of breaking through between Bras and Douaumont, and, by their attack on Verdun, of forcing the French to withdraw their wings, that they neglected first to attack the French positions on the left bank and in the Woevre plain, with the result that their colossal effort broke down before the tenacious resistance and heroism of the French.

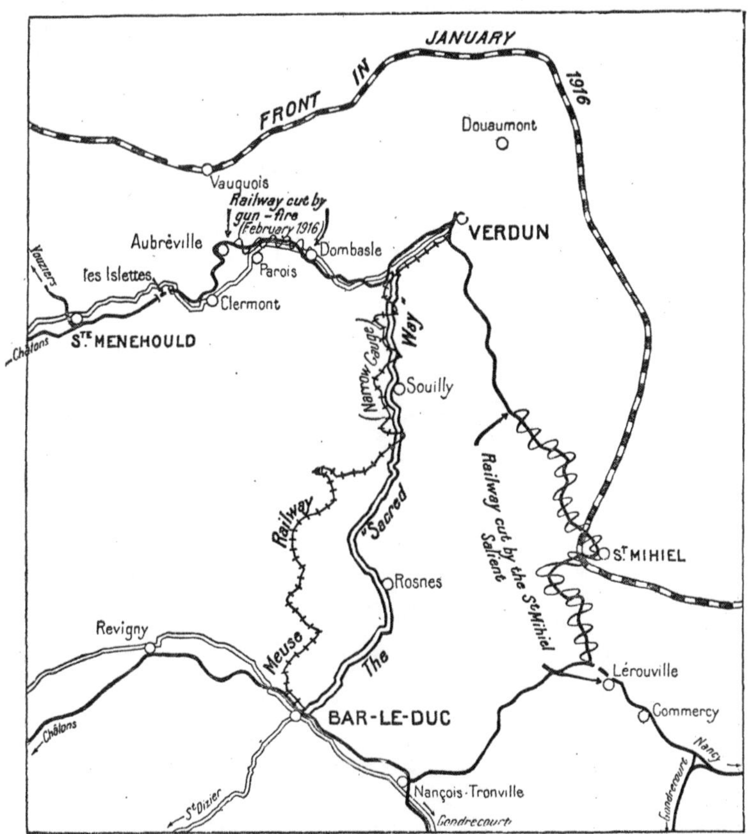

THE "SACRED WAY," AND THE NARROW-GAUGE MEUSE RAILWAY.

In February, 1916, *only one broad-gauge railway connected Verdun, via St. Menehould, with the rest of France. At the outset of the offensive it was cut by enemy gun-fire between Parois and Dombasle. There remained the narrow-gauge Meuse railway and the road. The carrying capacity of the former was increased to* 2,000 *tons per day, while the motor service along the "Sacred Way" was organised to such a pitch that it was able to ensure the transport of the troops, the evacuation of the wounded and the revictualling of* 250,000 *combatants.*

THE GERMAN OFFENSIVE

February–August, 1916

1.—The Central Attack

At the beginning of the battle, the first French lines were *on the left bank*, from Avocourt Wood to Forges, *via* the slopes in front of Malancourt and Béthincourt; *on the right bank*, from Brabant-sur-Meuse to Fromézey, *via* Haumont, Haumont Wood, Caures Wood, La Ville Wood, Herbébois, Ornes and Maucourt. On the morning of February 21st and simultaneously with a bombardment of the entire French front, the enemy began the systematic shelling of Verdun, whose last residents were evacuated on the 25th at noon.

The infantry attacked at 4.45 p.m. from Haumont Wood to Ornes. The 51st and 72nd divisions sustained the first shock of the IIIrd and XVIIIth C.A. and the XIIIth division of the VIIth R.C. A heroic combat followed the most formidable artillery preparation ever known till then. In Caures Wood the Chasseurs, under *Colonel Driant*, resisted foot by foot. When night fell, the enemy's progress was insignificant, compared with his sacrifices. However, they succeeded in taking Haumont Wood.

On the 22nd the bombardment was resumed with, if possible, greater intensity. In Caures Wood *Colonel Driant* resisted until death overtook him, having first evacuated his Chasseurs to Beaumont. Meanwhile, the sectors of Woevre and the left bank of the Meuse were violently shelled.

The fighting on the 23rd was even more furious. Brabant fell into the

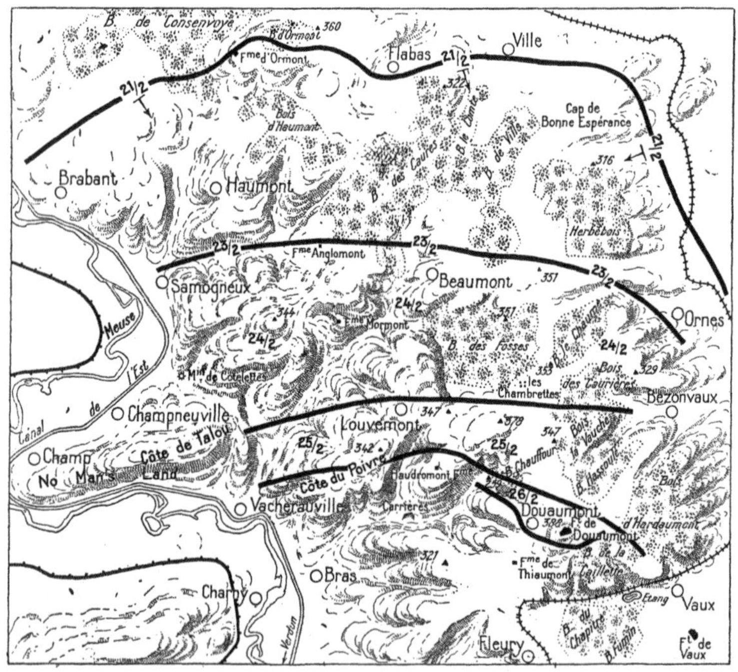

THE CENTRAL ATTACK.

This attack (February 21st–26th), on the right bank of the Meuse, shortened the enemy's front as progressed. It came to a stop on the sixth day at Poivre Hill and Douaumont.

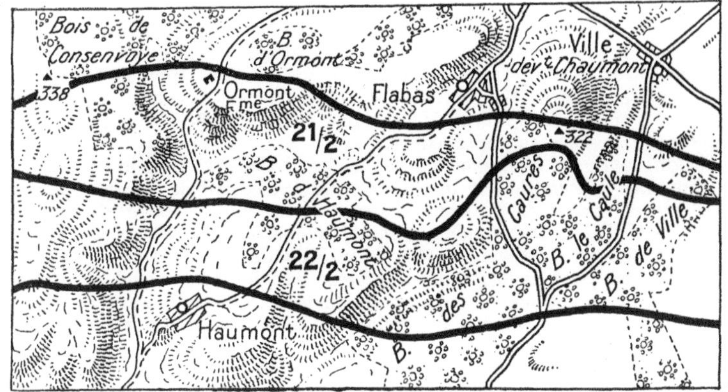

hands of the enemy after a fierce resistance by the 351st I.D., which clung desperately to the ruins of Samogneux until nightfall. Further east the battle raged fiercely. The French counter-attacked unsuccessfully at Caures Wood and were attacked at Herbebois. The 51st I.D. fell back, making the enemy pay dearly for his progress towards Fosses Wood.

In the evening the front extended along the Samogneux—Beaumont—Ornes line. Samogneux was captured by the enemy during the night. The situation was very critical.

Exasperated at the resistance of the French, and having received reinforcements, the Germans made a supreme effort on the 24th. Although harassed by French artillery on the left bank of the Meuse, they succeeded in taking Hill 344 to the east of Samogneux, Fosses Wood, Chaume Wood and the village of Ornes. French reinforcements arrived the same day, and the command of the army of Verdun passed from General de Castelnau to General Pétain.

On the 25th, the 37th I.D., with orders to defend Talou Hill and Louvemont village, resisted for a long time against incredibly furious attacks, but on their right the enemy succeeded in capturing Vauche Wood and, advancing

Starting-point of the German Attack of February 21st, North of Haumont Wood.

towards Douaumont, carried the fort by surprise. However, their efforts to take the village failed before the heroic tenacity of the 31st Brigade, while the 94th D.I. covered itself with glory. The enemy advance from this side, had the effect of compelling the 31st I.D. to abandon Talou Hill. During this time the line in Woevre was, unknown to the Germans, voluntarily withdrawn to the foot of the Meuse hills, where the French only retained outposts at Fresnes and Manheulles.

Taking over the command on the night of the 25th, General Pétain at once divided the battle-line into four sectors, officered as follows: *General Bazelaire*, on the left bank, from Avocourt to the river; *General Guillaumat*, from the Meuse to Douaumont; *General Balfourier*, from this point to the Woevre; *General Duchesne*, on the Meuse Heights.

There were no trenches, but he ordered that the forts should at least be connected by a continuous line of entrenchments to be made while the battle was at its height and which the "poilus," in their disdain for the shovel and pick, called the "Panic Line." The entire 59th division was told off to organise the counter slopes on the second and third lines. Thirteen battalions kept in repair the road from Bar-le-Duc to Verdun, *via* Souilly (the **"Sacred Way"**), which eventually became the main artery for revictualling the place in men and munitions, and along which 1,700 motor lorries passed each way daily. Lastly, General Pétain managed to imbue all under his command with his energy, activity and faith, and the enemy's drive was stopped.

On the 26th, the 39th D.I., which had relieved the 37th, victoriously repulsed all attacks on Poivre Hill, while the 31st Brigade continued to hold Douaumont until relieved in the evening by the 2nd D.I.

On the following days the fighting continued about and in the streets of Douaumont, which the enemy finally captured on March 4th. The Germans now began to show signs of weakening. Their effort on the right bank had

THE RELIEF BY MOTOR-LORRIES.

Regiment leaving Nixéville in lorries for the rear.

Mort-Homme and Hill 287 *in May,* 1916.

failed. Checked at Douaumont, they were taken in the rear by the French positions on the left bank, and were obliged to modify their plans. From that time they operated simultaneously or successively on both banks.

2.—The General Attack

(*See map, pp.* 14 *and* 15)

On March 6th two German divisions attacked from Béthincourt to Forges, where the French front was held by the 67th D.I., and succeeded in taking Forges and Regnéville, but were checked by the positions on Oie Hill. Continuing their advance on the 7th, they succeeded in capturing these positions, as well as Corbeaux Wood. The village of Cumières was the scene of terrible fighting, but remained in the hands of the French, while further to the west the enemy's attacks broke down at Mort-Homme.

On March 8th, while on the left bank, French troops retook Corbeaux Wood, the Germans brought into line units of five army corps and began a general attack, which failed with very heavy losses, their only gain being the capture of part of Vaux village.

On the 9th they succeeded in getting a footing on the slopes of Mort-Homme, but at the other end of the battle-line their attack on Vaux Fort failed. Their radiograms announcing the capture of the fort were untrue.

On the 10th, Corbeaux Wood was taken by the Germans and the French withdrew to the line Béthincourt, Mort-Homme, south of Corbeaux and Cumières Wood and Cumières village. The battle continued in the village and in front of Vaux Fort, strongly held by the French. The enemy temporarily ceased his massed attacks. In reality their offensive had failed, while their losses in men and munitions had been exceptionally heavy. On March 10th Joffre was able to say to the soldiers of Verdun : " *For three weeks you have withstood the most formidable attack which the enemy has yet made. Germany counted on the success of this effort, which she believed would prove irresistible, and for which she used her best troops and most powerful artillery. She hoped by the capture of Verdun to strengthen the courage of her Allies and convince neutrals of German superiority. But she reckoned without you! The eyes of the country are on you. You belong to those of whom it will be said : ' They barred the road to Verdun.'* "

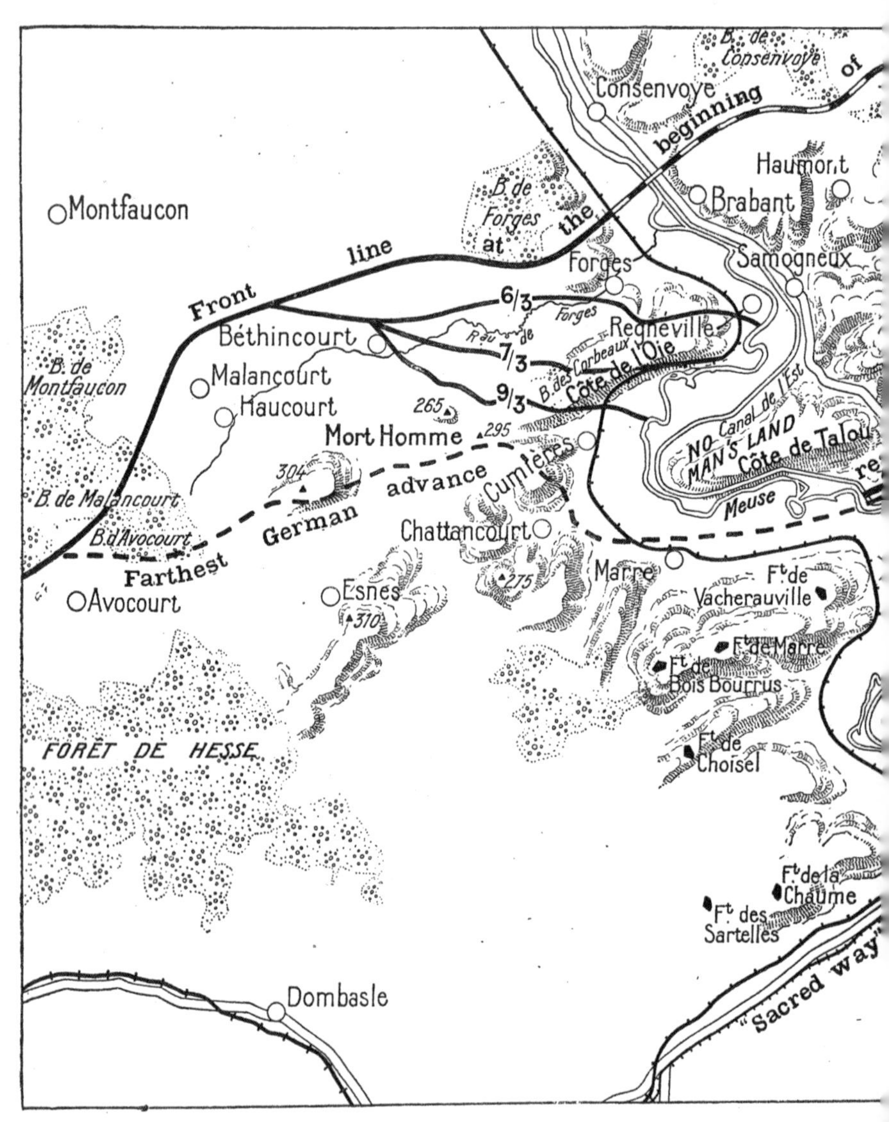

THE GERMAN GENERAL ATTAC

The Central Attack which was to capture Verdun and force back the French wings failed. The German both sides of the river. The struggle continued desperately at Mort-Homme, Hill 304, Cumière

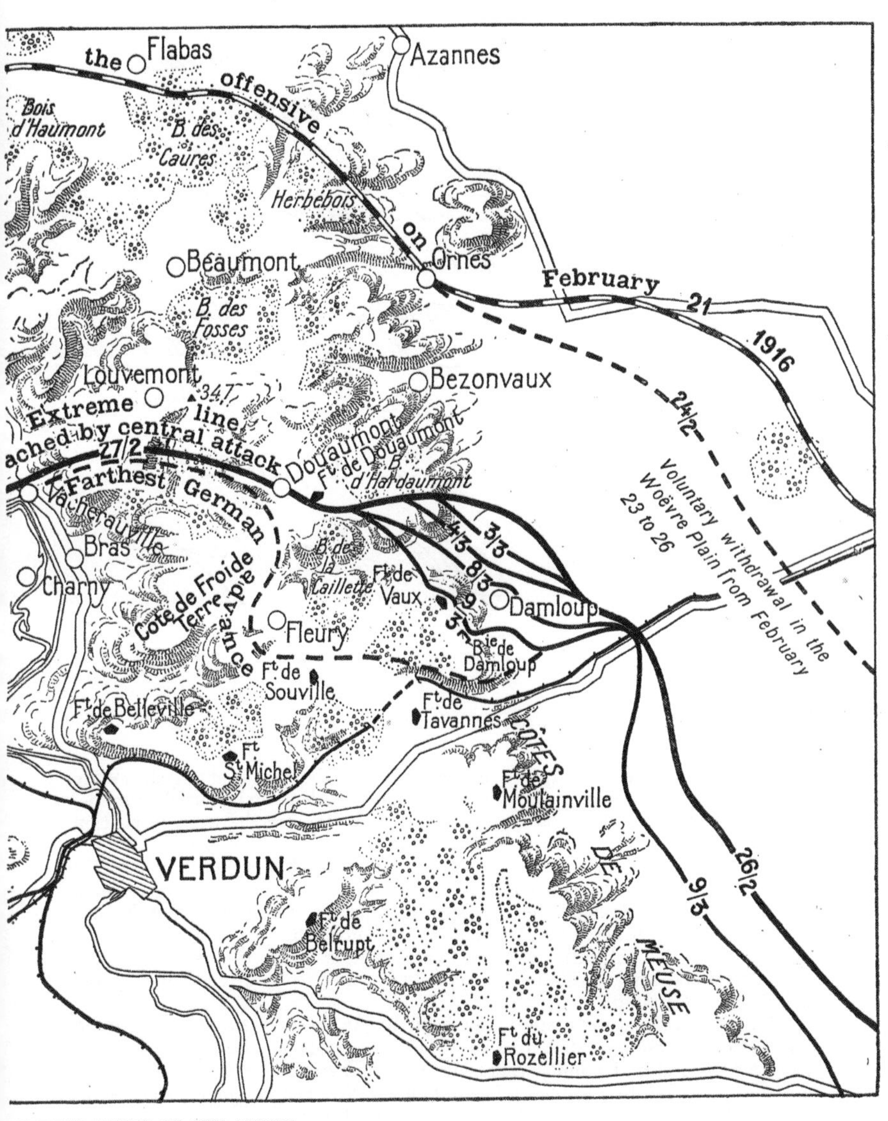

ON BOTH BANKS OF THE MEUSE.

caught on the flank by French artillery posted on the left bank of the Meuse, attacked alternately on Fleury, and as far as the approaches of Souville Fort—extreme limit of the German Advance in June, 1916.

Le 9 avril est une journée glorieuse pour nos armes.

Les assauts furieux des soldats du Kronprinz ont été partout brisés.

Fantassins, artilleurs, sapeurs, aviateurs de la 2e Armée ont rivalisé d'héroïsme.

Honneur à tous !

Les Allemands attaqueront sans doute encore. Que chacun travaille et veille pour obtenir le même succès qu'hier.

Courage... On les aura !

Ph. Pétain

GENERAL PÉTAIN'S ORDER OF THE DAY (*see translation below*).

From March 11th to April 9th the aspect of the battle changed. Wide front attacks gave place to local actions, short, violent and limited in scope. On March 14th the Germans captured Hill 265, forming the western portion of the Mort-Homme position, from the 75th French Brigade, whose commander Colonel Garçon, fell, rifle in hand, but they failed to take the eastern part, Hill 295. On the 20th, Avocourt and Malancourt Woods fell to the Bavarians, and after a fierce struggle the village of Malancourt was lost on March 31st, Haucourt on April 5th, and Béthincourt on April 8th.

On the right bank, after powerful attacks near Vaux, the enemy reached Caillette Wood and the Vaux-Fleury railway, only to be driven back by the 5th division (Mangin).

A furious attack was made along both banks by the Germans at noon on April 9th ; *on the left bank*, five divisions were engaged, failing everywhere except at the Mort-Homme, where, despite the heroic resistance of the 42nd division (Deville), they gained a footing on the N.E. slopes ; *on the right bank*, Poivre Hill was attacked but remained in French hands.

"*April 9th was a glorious day for our armies*," General Pétain declared in his order of the day dated the 10th, "*the furious attacks of the soldiers of the Crown Prince broke down everywhere. The infantry, artillery, sappers and aviators of the 2nd Army vied with one another in valour. Honour to all. No doubt the Germans will attack again. Let all work and watch, that yesterday's success be continued. Courage ! We shall beat them !*"

General Nivelle, taking over the Command of Verdun Army in May, 1916.

On the 10th the enemy continued his efforts with small success.

From that date operations were limited to local actions, either in reply to French counter-offensives (attacks of April 11th between Douaumont

Entrance to Douaumont Fort,

and Vaux and between the Meuse and Douaumont on the 17th), or in endeavours to take key positions where the French offered vigorous resistance. At the beginning of May General Pétain, having received the command of the central group of armies, General Nivelle took over that of the army of Verdun.

From May 4th to 24th the Germans attacked furiously around Mort-Homme. On the 4th they captured the northern slopes of Hill 304, where desperate combats took place on the 5th and 6th. By a powerful attack on the 7th they forced the French to abandon the crest of Hill 304, which, however, they were unable to occupy on account of the violence of the bombardment. Cumières and Caurettes fell on the 24th.

In the meantime, the battle had started afresh on the Douaumont—Vaux front. On May 22nd, at 11.50 a.m., the French 5th D.I. attacked and recaptured the fort of Douaumont, the casemates of which were the scene of desperate hand-to-hand fighting. The French were driven out on the 24th, but maintained their positions in the immediate vicinity.

The battle continued without respite or quarter. Not an hour passed without a surprise of some sort being attempted. The Germans were determined to advance, but at every step they were checked by the unflinching will of the French not to let them pass.

From May 29th to 31st the enemy attacked Hill 304 and at Mort-Homme. June 1st was marked by the loss of the Hardaumont salient and Thiaumont Farm. On the 2nd the enemy progressed in Fumin Wood, but lost Thiaumont Farm. On the 3rd they gained a footing in Vaux Fort, which was entirely in their possession on the 8th. On the 9th they attacked Hill 304 and Damloup Battery and retook Thiaumont Farm. On the 12th they advanced along La Dame Ravine, but lost the N.E. slopes of Mort-Homme on the 15th.

On the 23rd, after an uninterrupted bombardment, begun the day before, the Germans launched their greatest attack. Seventeen regiments were hurled simultaneously against the Thiaumont—Fleury—Souville front, resulting in the capture of the Thiaumont redoubt and the gaining of a footing in the village of Fleury, but failing to take the fort of Souville.

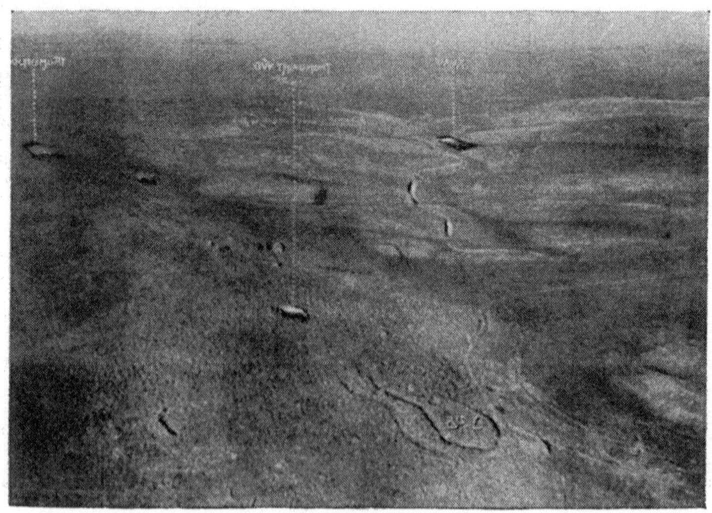

Aspect of the Battlefield in July, 1916.

Froide-Terre Hill, momentarily invaded, was cleared of the enemy by a grenade and bayonet attack.

On the following days, the fighting centred around the Thiaumont redoubt, which changed hands many times, remaining finally with the enemy on June 30th.

Combats, frequent and furious, continued on both banks until the middle of August.

FRENCH COUNTER-OFFENSIVES—CLEARING VERDUN

October–December, 1916–*August*, 1917

The French Offensive of October 24th, 1916, on the Right Bank of the Meuse

From August, 1916, the Germans, in consequence of the Franco-British offensive in the Somme, gradually abandoned Verdun, in which venture she

General Mangin in front of his Post of Commandment.

had sacrificed the pick of her troops. The army of Verdun took advantage of this to regain the initiative of the operations.

Under the command of General Mangin the French attacked from Thiaumont to Laufée Wood on October 24th, 1916, the artillery preparation by 650 guns, including the new 15-inch and 16-inch mortars, beginning on October 20th. On the 22nd a feint attack enabled French aeroplanes to locate 158 enemy batteries, which were heavily shelled the next day.

That the Germans did not realise the position was evident from the Crown Prince's announcement that he had broken a strong French attack. The real attack took place on the morning of the 24th (*see map, p.* 20).

The German front was held on the first line by seven divisions. The French attacked with three divisions: the 38th (Guyot de Salins), supported on the left by the 11th line regiment; the 133rd (Passaga), known as "La Gauloise"; the 74th (de Lardemelle).

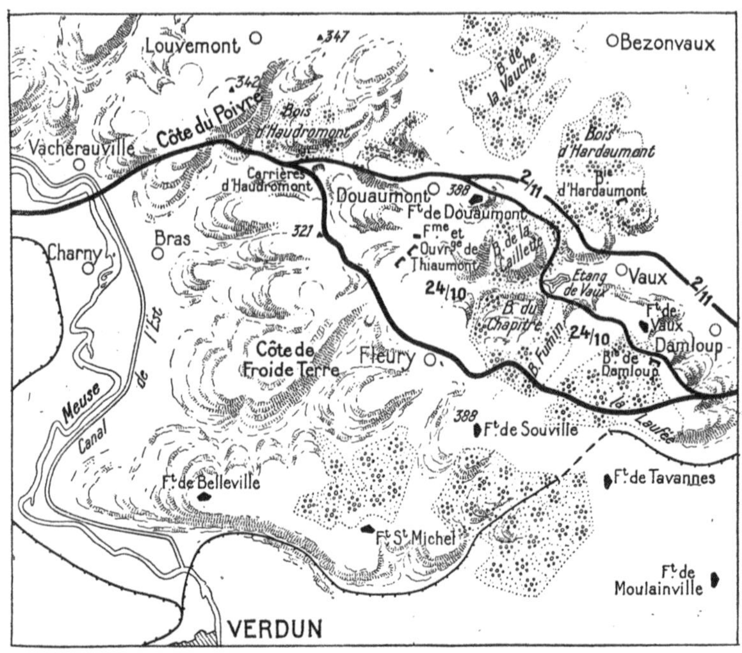

The attack was a brilliant success and gave the French the Haudromont quarries, Thiaumont redoubt and farm, Douaumont fort and village, the northern edge of Caillette Wood, Vaux pond, the eastern edge of Fumin Wood and Damloup battery. On the 24th and 25th more than 6,000 prisoners, fifteen guns, and considerable quantities of material, were captured. On November 2nd, when the French re-entered Vaux Fort, abandoned by the enemy, they practically re-occupied their positions of February 24th.

The Approaches of Tavannes Fort.

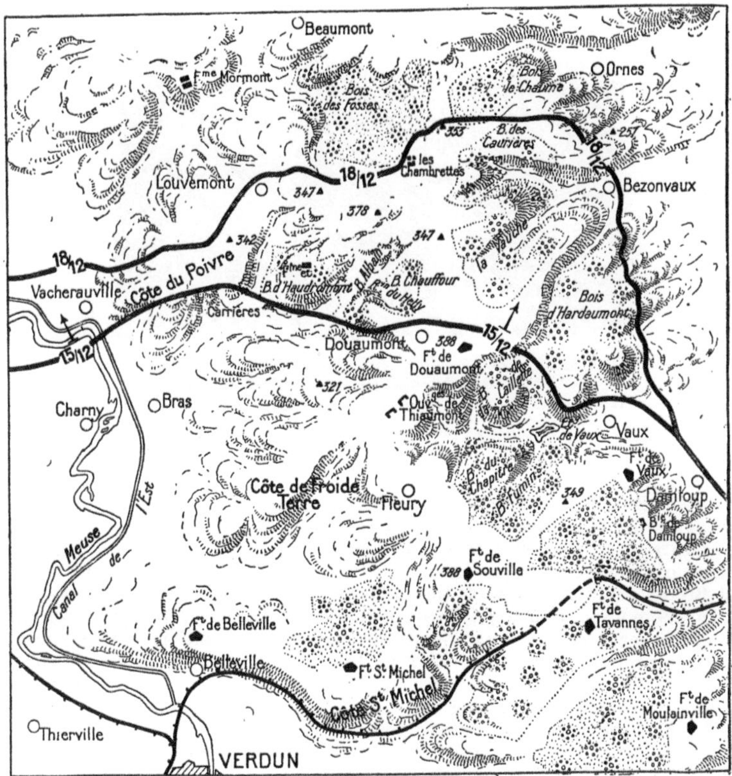

The French Offensive of December 15th, 1916, on the Right Bank of the Meuse

To completely clear Verdun to the east of the Meuse and give greater freedom to the reconquered forts of Vaux and Douaumont, General Mangin organised a new attack. A great amount of preparatory work was done by the army of Verdun, including about eighteen miles of road (whereof one of logs laid transversely for the artillery), more than six miles of narrow-gauge railway, and a network of trenches and depots for munitions and material. As soon as these very considerable preparations, often carried out under heavy enemy shell-fire, were finished, the attacking troops took up their positions: the 126th D.I. (Muteau), 38th D.I. (Guyot de Salins), 37th D.I. (Garnier-Duplessis) and 133rd D.I. (Passaga), with the 123rd, 128th, 21st and 6th D.I. as reserves. Two lines of artillery prepared and sustained the attack: one from Vacherauville to Thiaumont, Fleury and Souville, the other passing through Belleville, St. Michel Hill and Tavannes Fort. The six-mile German front from Vacherauville to Bezonvaux was held by five divisions in the first line, with four divisions in reserve.

On December 15th, while Germany was proposing that France should ask for peace, the reply came in the form of attacking waves protected by a moving curtain of artillery fire.

Several of the objectives, including Vacherauville, Poivre Hill, Hill 342 and the first and second lines before Louvemont, were reached in a few minutes

Hill 304 recaptured. (*Photographed August 24th*, 1917. *See p.* 24)

at a single bound. Albain and Chauffour Woods, those in front of Douaumont and Helly Ravine, took longer to capture. To the east La Vauche Wood was carried at the point of the bayonet, Caurières Wood passed, and the edges of Chaume Wood reached. The farm of Les Chambrettes and village of Bezonvaux were taken on the following days. The success was considerable, more than 11,000 prisoners, including 300 officers, 115 guns, several hundred machine-guns and important depots of munitions and material, being captured. The enemy who, in July, had been within a few hundred yards of Souville Fort, was now more than three miles away. In June, the *Frankfort Gazette*, celebrating the German successes at Verdun, declared: "We have clinched our victory and none can take it from us," but on December 18th they had lost all the ground it had taken five months and enormous sacrifices to conquer.

In congratulating the troops General Mangin reminded them that Germany had just invited France to sue for peace, adding that they had been "the true ambassadors of the Republic."

Fontaines Ravine, West of Bezonvaux.

The French Offensive of August 20th, 1917

The Army of Verdun, under General Guillaumat, completed the clearing of the city on both banks of the Meuse.

On August 20th, 1917, eight divisions attacked from Avocourt Wood on

General Guillaumat

the west to Bezonvaux on the east, along a fifteen-mile front. Avocourt Wood, Mort-Homme, Corbeaux Wood and Oie Hill on the left bank; Talou Hill, the villages of Champ, Neuville and Champneuville, Hill 344, parts of Fosses Wood, Chaume Wood and Mormont Farm, on the right bank, were captured

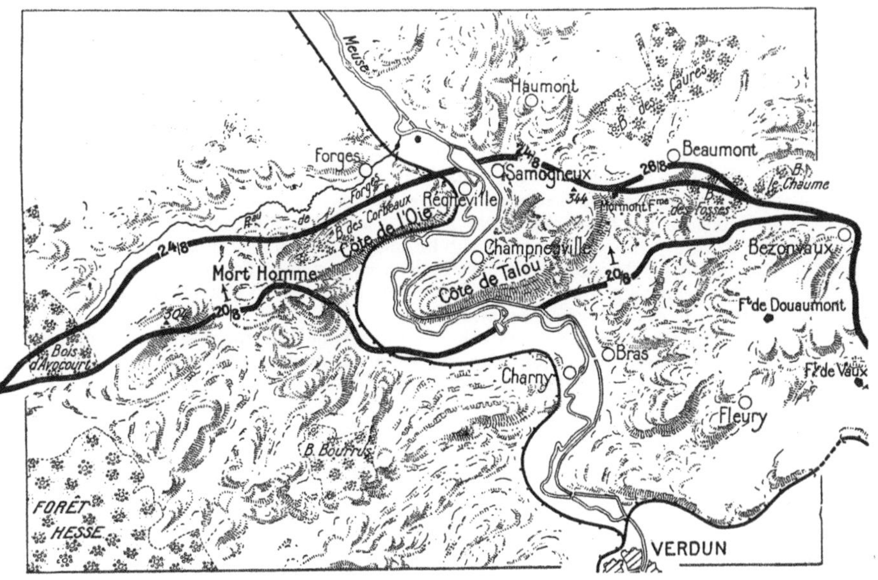

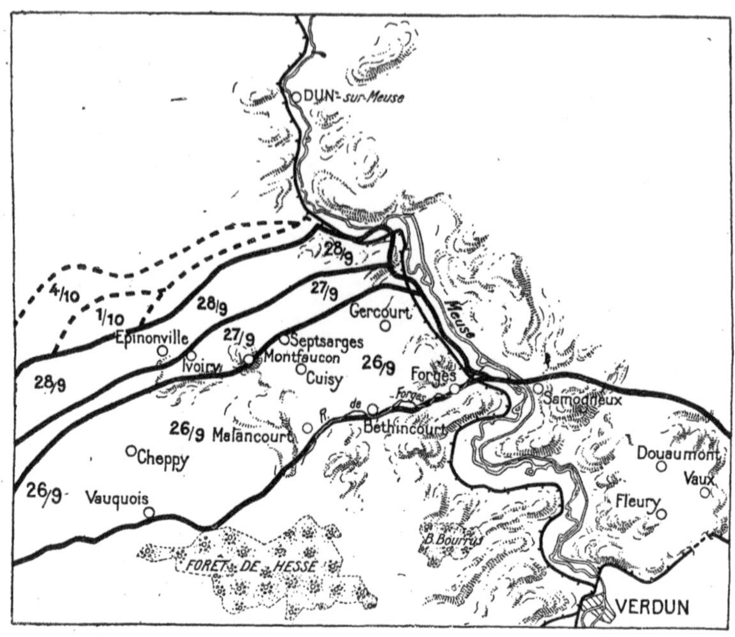

by the French, who, the next day, also took Samogneux and Regneville. Hill 304, which had thus far resisted, was likewise captured. On the 26th a further attack from Mormont Redoubt to Chaume Wood brought the French to the southern outskirts of Beaumont. From the 20th to the 26th August the captures include 9,500 prisoners, thirty guns, 100 trench mortars and 242 machine-guns.

The American Offensive of September 26th, 1918

(*See Panorama, pp.* 106 *and* 107)

The clearing of Verdun was entirely and definitely effected in the autumn of 1918.

While the 4th French Army, under General Gouraud, attacked between the Moronvillers Hills and Argonne on September 26th, the American Army, under General Pershing, took the offensive between the Argonne and the Meuse.

Artillery preparation commenced at 2.30 a.m. and lasted three hours. At 5.30 a.m. the Americans attacked with great dash the redoubtable enemy positions on the left bank of the Meuse, capturing Malancourt, Béthincourt and Forges. Keeping up with the infantry, the artillery crossed the Forges stream during the morning. The woods, very strongly defended, were cleared of the enemy, and by noon the Americans had reached Gercourt, Cuisy, the southern part of Montfaucon and Cheppy.

In the afternoon a desperate battle was engaged on the positions covering the redoubtable ridge of Montfaucon, the most important enemy observation-post in the region of Verdun. The Americans wisely turned the ridge on the right, advancing as far as Septsarges. By evening Montfaucon was surrounded. The advance, now slower, continued on the 27th and 28th, despite German counter-attacks. To the west of Montfaucon, Ivoiry and Epinonville were captured, and thus the ridge fell. The Americans took 8,000 prisoners and 100 guns.

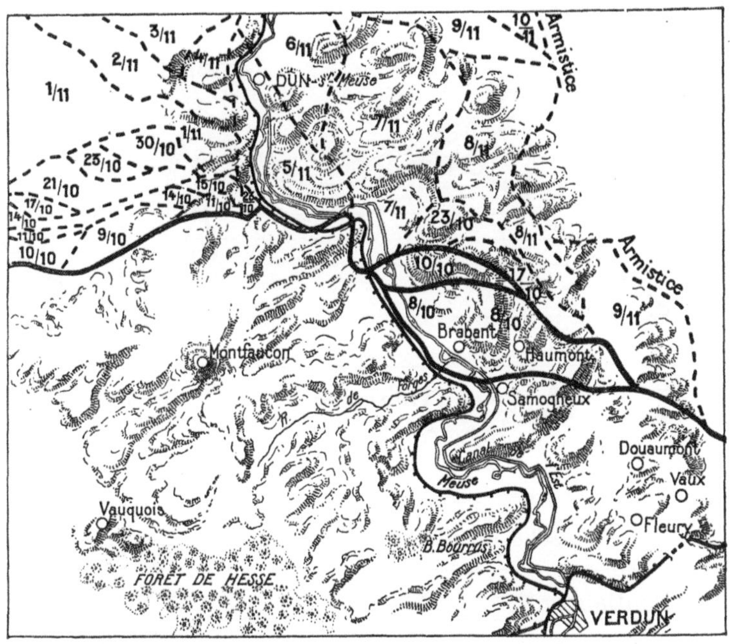

The Francc-American Offensive of October, 1918

On the right bank of the Meuse, a French army corps and American troops, under General Pershing, joined in the struggle, capturing Brabant, Haumont, Haumont Wood and Caures Wood, while the famous line from which, in February, 1916, the Crown Prince's army had attacked Verdun, was soon reached and passed. By the end of October more than 20,000 prisoners, 150 guns, nearly 1,000 trench-mortars and several thousand machine-guns, had been captured, while unconquered Verdun was definitely lost to the Germans Their retreat was now destined to continue uninterruptedly until the Armistice.

Renault Tanks and American Troops on the old French Lines at Regnéville.

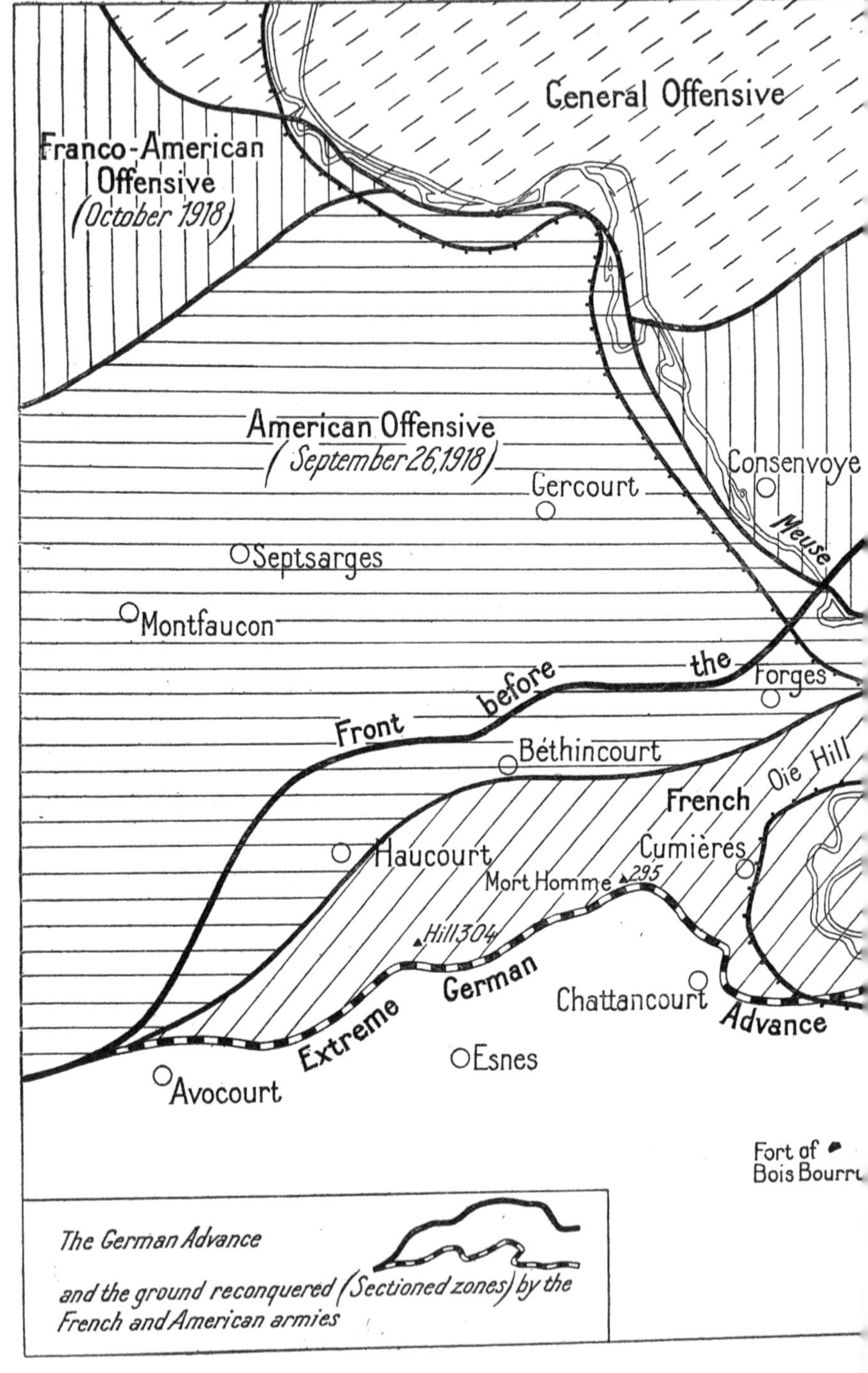
General Offensive
Franco-American Offensive (October 1918)
American Offensive (September 26, 1918)
Consenvoye
Gercourt
Meuse
Septsarges
Montfaucon
Front before the French
Forges
Béthincourt
Oie Hill
Haucourt
Cumières
Mort Homme 295
Hill 304
Extreme German Advance
Chattancourt
Esnes
Avocourt
Fort of Bois Bourrus
The German Advance
and the ground reconquered (Sectioned zones) by the French and American armies

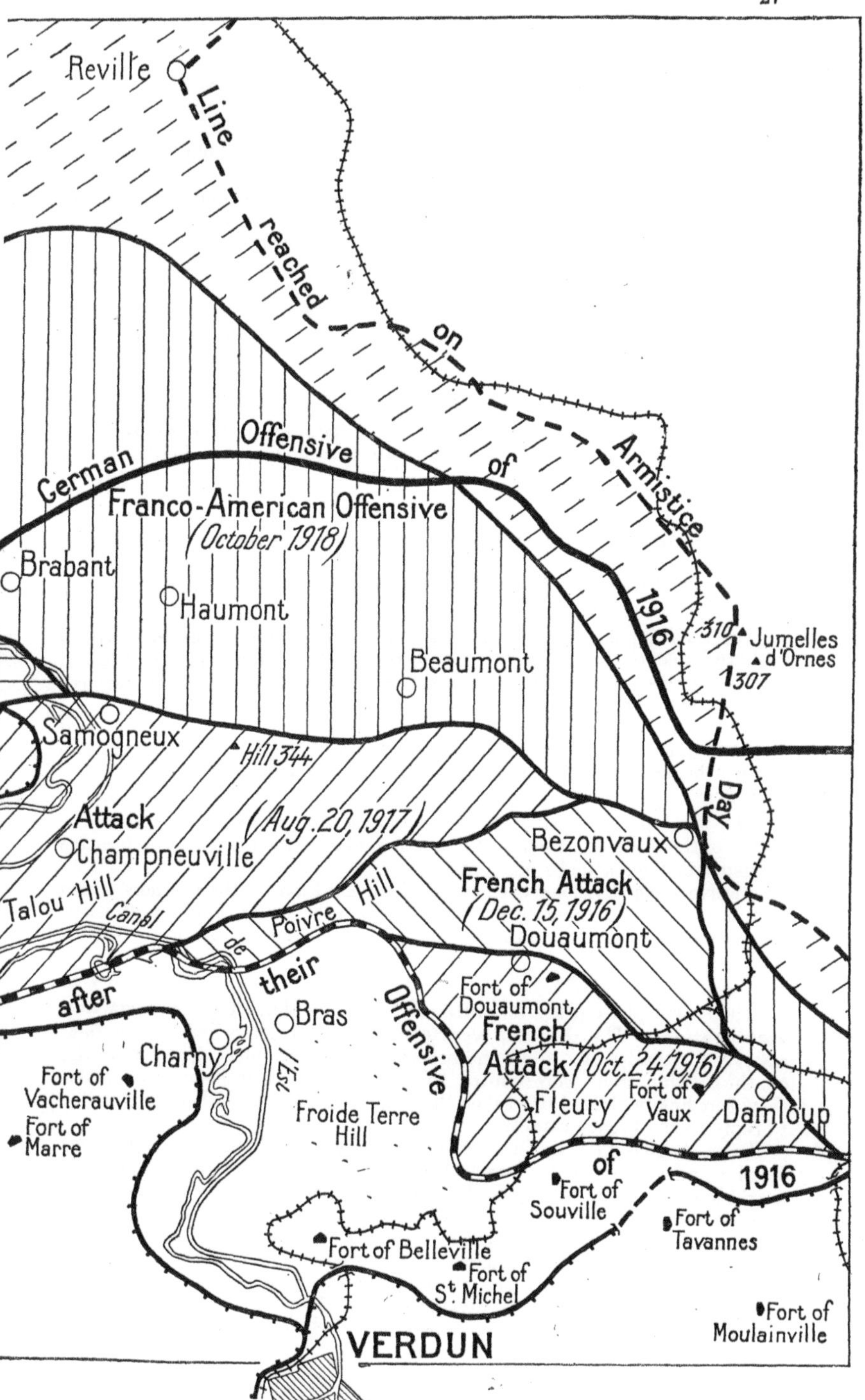
Reville
Line reached on Armistice Day
German Offensive of 1916
Franco-American Offensive
(October 1918)
Brabant
Haumont
Beaumont
310
307
Jumelles d'Ornes
Samogneux
Hill 344
Attack (Aug. 20, 1917)
Champneuville
Talou Hill
Bezonvaux
French Attack
(Dec. 15, 1916)
Poivre Hill
Canal de l'Est
Douaumont
Fort of Douaumont
after their Offensive of 1916
Bras
Charny
French Attack (Oct. 24, 1916)
Fort of Vacherauville
Fort of Marre
Froide Terre Hill
Fleury
Fort of Vaux
Damloup
Fort of Souville
Fort of Tavannes
Fort of Belleville
Fort of St. Michel
Fort of Moulainville
VERDUN

CONCLUSION

The Battle of Verdun was not merely one of the hardest of the War's many battles, it was also one of the most serious checks received by the Germans. The enemy High Command had foreseen neither its amplitude nor its long duration. Whereas, "according to plan," Verdun—"Heart of France"—was speedily to be overpowered by a carefully prepared mass attack, the Germans found themselves involved in a formidable struggle, without being able either to obtain a decisive advantage or keep the relatively small advantages obtained at the beginning of the battle.

The battle did not develop "according to plan," its successive phases being determined by circumstances.

The huge numbers of troops which the Germans were compelled to engage brings out very clearly the immensity of their effort and the different phases of the struggle.

The first and shortest phase (February 21st–March 1st) was that of the **surprise attack** by a large concentration of specially trained troops.

To the six German divisions which had been holding the Verdun sector since the Battle of the Marne, were added nine full divisions, rested and trained for attack.

Of these fifteen divisions ten took part in the surprise attack, their losses being immediately made good by reserves stationed in the rear of each army corps. At the end of February, in consequence of the French withdrawal in Woevre, two further divisions strengthened enemy action in that region.

The second phase (March 2nd–April 15th) marked the **general attack** on both banks of the Meuse, in place of the surprise attack which had failed.

During this period nine and a half fresh German divisions were engaged, of which four came from the Eastern front.

At the same time two and a half German divisions were withdrawn and rested in quiet sectors, while four others were sent to the rear to reform, two of them being, however, again engaged after twenty days' rest.

The third phase (April 15th–July 1st) was that of **attrition.** After the failure of their general attack and to avoid avowal of their defeat, the Germans persisted in their attacks on Verdun.

Twelve fresh divisions were engaged, in addition to three others which had been sent to the rear to reform. On the other hand, fourteen divisions were withdrawn and sent to the rear, to Russia, or other sectors on the French front.

The fourth phase (July 1st, 1916, to 1917) was that of the **retreat and stabilisation.** The Germans were exhausted and compelled to use their reserves for the Russian front and especially in the Somme. Their activities on the Verdun front were limited to making good their losses. However, they were finally obliged to weaken this front to a point that they were unable to reply to the French attacks.

From August 21st to October 1st, the Germans brought up only one division and withdrew four. From October 1st to 24th, three divisions relieved nearly five. After October 24th the strength of the enemy forces varied only slightly, the French offensives preventing any further weakening of the front. The attrition caused by the French attacks of October 24th and December 15th gave rise only to rapid replacements of about equal importance.

In brief, from February 21st, 1916, to February 1st, 1917, the Germans engaged fifty-six and a half divisions (or 567 battalions), of which six divisions appeared successively on both banks of the Meuse, eight others being

Douaumont Fort and its Approaches.
(Photographed from aeroplane in May, 1916.)

also engaged twice and six three times. In reality, in the course of eleven months, eighty-two and a half German divisions took part in the attacks on Verdun, which they had expected to crush in a few days with ten to twelve divisions. The contrast between this formidable effort and the meagre results obtained is striking, and is a splendid testimony to the courage and tenacity of the defenders. The Battle of Verdun in 1916 was not merely a severe local setback for the Germans ; by using up their best troops it had also very important strategical consequences. Their successes were few, temporary, and dearly bought Advancing painfully, each step forward was marked by a mountain of corpses. Up to the end of the War, even after the Battles of the Somme and Aisne in 1916 and 1917, and after the Battle of Champagne in 1918, Verdun remained a hideous spectre for the German people, while their soldiers surnamed it **"The Slaughter-House of Germany."**

As the French President, M. Poincaré, declared, on handing to the Mayor of Verdun the decorations conferred on that city by the Allied nations, it was before the walls of Verdun that " the supreme hope of Imperial Germany was crushed." It was at Verdun that Germany sought the " kolossal " victory which was to enslave the world, and it was there that France quietly but firmly replied " No road." For centuries to come the name of Verdun will continue to ring in the ears of humanity like a shout of victory and a cry of deliverance.

Verdun Decorated

It was in a casemate of the Citadel, transformed into a *salle de fêtes*, that, on September 13th, 1916, Président Poincaré handed the undermentioned decorations, conferred on the city by the Chiefs of State of the Allied countries, to the Municipal Authorities of Verdun: St. George's Cross of Russia (white enamel); the British Military Cross (silver); the medal for military valour of Italy (gold); the Cross of Leopold I. of Belgium (gold); the medal " Ohilitch " of Montenegro (gold); the " Croix de la Légion d'Honneur " and the " Croix de Guerre " of France. Since then the French Government has conferred a Sword of Honour on the city. Generals Joffre, Pétain and Nivelle, the Military Governor (General Dubois), the French War Minister and representatives of the Allied Nations were present at this moving ceremony, which consecrated the heroic resistance of the army of Verdun and the German defeat.

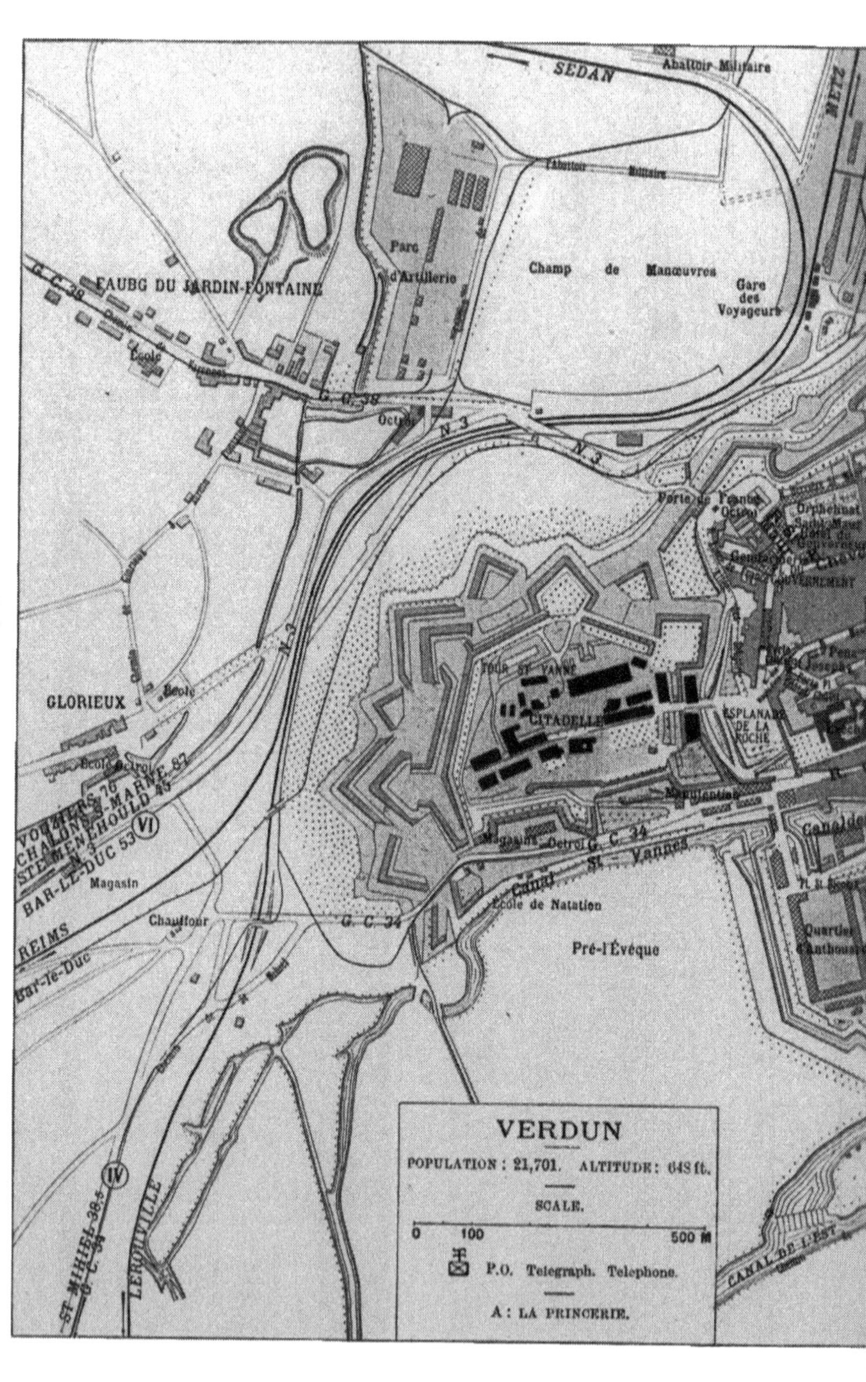
SEDAN
Abattoir Militaire
METZ
Parc
d'Artillerie
Champ de Manœuvres
Gare
des
Voyageurs
FAUBG DU JARDIN-FONTAINE
G. C. 38
École
Octroi
N. 3
Porte de France
Orphelinat
GOUVERNEMENT
N. 3
TOUR ST VANNE
CITADELLE
ESPLANADE
DE LA
ROCHE
GLORIEUX
École
École Octroi
VOUZIERS 76
CHALONS-S-MARNE 87
STE MENEHOULD 49
VI
N. 3
BAR-LE-DUC 53
Magasin
Manutention
Magasins
Octroi
G. C. 34
Canal
St Vannes
École de Natation
Chauffour
G. C. 34
Pré-l'Évêque
Quartier
d'Anthouard
REIMS
Bar-le-Duc
IV
ST MIHIEL 36.5
G. C. 34
LEROUVILLE
CANAL DE L'EST
VERDUN
POPULATION : 21,701. ALTITUDE : 648 ft.
SCALE.
0 100 500 M
P.O. Telegraph. Telephone.
A : LA PRINCERIE.

Etang
Av. Miribel
I. C. 11
Caserne Miribel
Baraquement du Faubourg Pavé
FAUBG DU PAVE
Magasins à Fourrages
École
Route d'Etain
École St Jean Baptiste
N 18
BRIEY 44
ETAIN 20
Cimetière Israélite
Le Coulmier
MEUSE
ST SAUVEUR
Congrégation Notre-Dame
PL. DU MARCHÉ
Courtine 16
Octroi
St Victor
Kiosque
Temple Protestant
N 64
N 3
METZ 63
NANCY 96.5
TOUL 77
COMMERCY 53

A VISIT TO THE CITY OF VERDUN

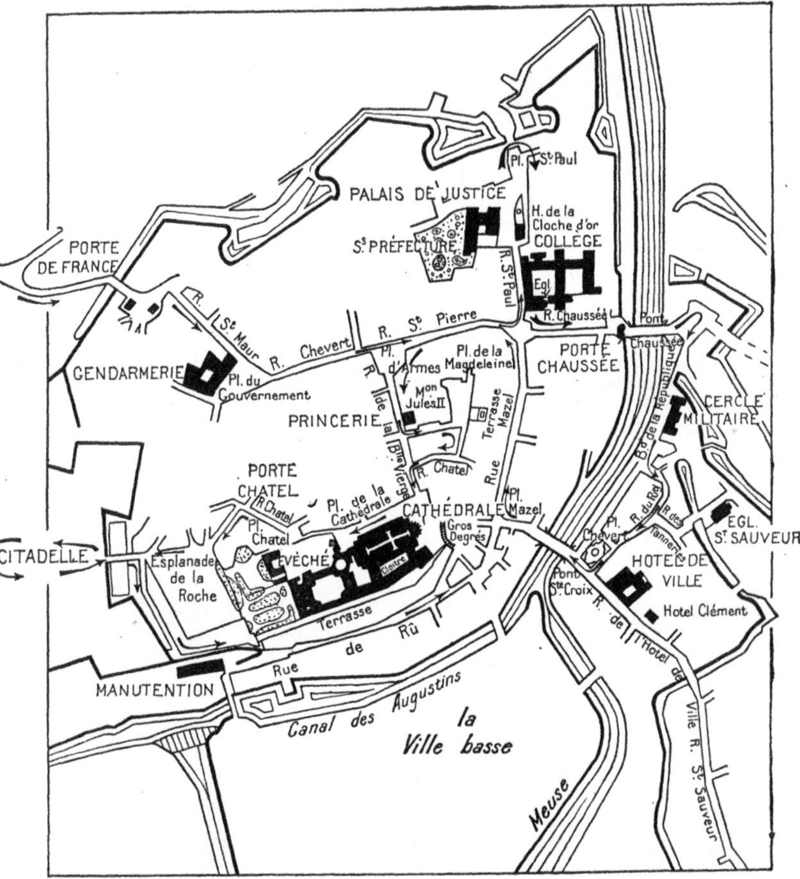

Motorists coming either from St. Menehould, or Bar-le-Duc, via the **"Sacred Way,"** *enter Verdun by the Porte-de-France, which has been chosen as the starting-point of the following descriptive itinerary for visiting the town. Follow the* **streets shown on the outline map,** *in the direction of the* **arrows,** *consulting at the same time the* **text** *and* **photographs** *on pp. 32-56.*

See also the **two-coloured plan** *opposite.*

VISIT TO THE CITY

From the **Porte-de-France,** whose entrance arcade on the bridge dates from Louis XIV., *take the Rue St. Maur, leading to the Place du Gouvernement.*

THE PLACE D'ARMES

This square owes its name to the building called "Le Gouvernement," or "Ancien Logis du Roi." Residence of the War Minister, M. Louvois, in 1687, and to-day a barracks for the gendarmes. It was damaged by the bombardment.

From the Place du Gouvernement go via *the Rue Chevert to the Place d'Armes.*

The **Place d'Armes,** badly damaged by bombardment, occupies the site of a tower (Tour le Princier) of the old rampart.

Go down the Rue St. Pierre.

RUE ST. PIERRE IN 1916.

In background RUE CHAUSSÉE. *On the right:* RUE MAZEL.

Turning to the left into the Rue St. Paul, the tourist passes in front of **the College.**

The present building was erected in 1890 on the site of the old college, founded in 1570 by Bishop Nicolas Psaume in the grounds of the ancient Hôpital de St. Nicolas-de-Gravière. Its church, a fine Ionic structure, was built in 1730 by the Jesuits. The college was one of the first buildings to be damaged by the bombardment, being struck in 1915, prior to the great German offensive against Verdun.

Continue along Rue St. Paul as far as the **Palais de Justice** *and the* **Sub-Préfecture** (*photo, p.* 34).

These two buildings are the remains of the second Abbey of the Premonstrants of St. Paul, built inside the town after 1552. The first, situated without the walls, was destroyed by order of the Military Authorities, who feared a siege by Charles Quint.

In the SOUS-PRÉFECTURE vestiges of the ancient monastery are more numerous and apparent. The *Salle des Archives*, with its slender columns and great Renaissance bays, was the monks' refectory. The *Cabinet du Sous-Préfet*, with its austere vaulting, has retained its archaic appearance. In the *Loge du Concierge* (caretaker's lodge) there still exists one of the original mantelpieces, with carving representing Abraham sacrificing Isaac. The marble-paved *vestibule* and fine *staircase* are also 16th century.

The interior arrangement of the Palais de Justice buildings, whose façade is ornamented with a finely carved semicircular *pediment*, has been changed. Of the old convent there now only remains the Salle des Pas-Perdus, formerly the cloister.

The **Hôtel de la Cloche d'Or,** near by, has been installed in the ancient "Procure" of the same monastery (St. Paul's).

FAÇADE OF COLLEGE CHURCH, RUE ST. PAUL, MAY, 1919.

INTERIOR OF COLLEGE CHURCH.
Photographed in May, 1919.

THE PALAIS DE JUSTICE

The books and woodwork of the monastery have been removed to the Municipal Library.

Return by the Rue St. Paul to the Rue Chaussée, into which turn to the left ; at the end is the **Chaussée Gate** (*hist. mon.*), built about 1380 (*see pp.* 35 *and* 58).

Its architecture recalls that of the Bastille. Half of the left tower on the river was rebuilt in 1690, exactly on the same lines and with the stones of the old tower ; the semicircular arcade and the pediment facing the bridge are of the same date.

The pediment between the two towers was struck by shell splinters, otherwise the bombardments did not damage the gate.

THE BANKS OF THE MEUSE AND THE CATHEDRAL BEFORE THE WAR.

(*Compare with photos on pp.* 35 *and* 37)

THE CHAUSSÉE GATE (before the War)

Cross the Chaussée Bridge over the Meuse, then take on the right the Boulevard de la République, which passes in front of the Cercle Militaire (Military Club).

THE BANKS OF THE MEUSE, THE CATHEDRAL AND ST. CROIX BRIDGE.

Photographed from the Military Club in May, 1919.

ST. SAVIOUR'S CHURCH.

Take on the left the Rue du Puty and the Rue des Tanneries, then the Minimes Bridge (also on the left), at the end of which is **St. Saviour's Church.**

The church is modern, having replaced the old Eglise des Minimes in 1830. It contains, however, some interesting stained-glass windows, while at the entrance is the tomb of the founder of the old church, Bishop Bousnard, deceased in 1584.

Return by the Rue des Tanneries to the Rue du Puty, turn to the left, reaching the **Place Chevert** *on the right bank of the Meuse* (*see photo, p.* 37).

There is a fine view of the upper town, bishop's palace and cathedral from this square. The latter was begun in 1552, after the Church of St. Croix had been pulled down. A statue of *General Chevert*, by the sculptor of the pediment of the Madeleine in Paris (Lemaire), has been erected on the site of this church. In December, 1916, this statue was removed to the underground vaults of the Citadelle.

THE INTERIOR OF ST. SAVIOUR'S CHURCH.

CHEVERT SQUARE AND STATUE OF GENERAL CHEVERT.

(Born at Verdun in 1695, General Chevert captured Prague in 1741. After a heroic defence, he capitulated in 1743, with the honours of War.)

THE MEUSE (SEEN FROM CHEVERT SQUARE, 1916).

On the other side of Chevert Square is the Rue de l'Hôtel-de-Ville, which ends on the right at St. Croix Bridge. Follow it on the left as far as the **Hôtel-de-Ville** (*see Itinerary, p.* 31).

FAÇADE OF THE HÔTEL-DE-VILLE OVERLOOKING THE GARDENS. (May 1919)

Hôtel-de-Ville

As one of the lofty windows bears the date 1623, the popular belief that the building was erected by the famous Governor Marillac is unfounded. It is possible, however, that tradition, according to which Marillac sheltered Marie de Médicis there, after her flight from Paris, is founded on fact.

It is a fine structure in the Medicis style. The façade which overlooks the garden resembles that of the Luxembourg in Paris in some of its lines.

At the side of the Hôtel-de-Ville, at No. 19, *is the house of M. Clement.*

A learned amateur, Monsieur Clément, who was killed during the bombardments of 1916, had collected a considerable number of fragments of the Abbey of St. Vanne and rebuilt the principal doorway of the latter (*see p.* 52) in the courtyard of his house. The famous door of the Capitulary Room, described

MAIN ENTRANCE (REBUILT) TO THE ABBEY OF ST. VANNE, IN THE COURT OF NO. 19 RUE DE L'HÔTEL-DE-VILLE

and drawn by Viollet-le-Duc, was of curious 13th-century design. The lintel of the tympanum was ornamented with foliage, which is an interesting peculiarity, as the sculptural decoration of the tympanums of doors was very rare at that time in civil architecture.

RUINS IN THE RUE MAZEL AND RUE DU ST. ESPRIT.

Return to the Place Chevert, cross the St. Croix Bridge, and go to the Place d'Armes via *the Place and Rue Mazel,* whose houses are in ruins.

THE PRINCERIE IN 1916, RUE DE LA BELLE-VIERGE, NOS. 16 AND 18 (*see p.* 40).

Turn to the left into the Rue St. Pierre. In the Place d'Armes take the Rue de la Belle-Vierge as far as the **Hôtel de la Princerie,** former residence of the "primicerius," first archdeacon of the Cathedral.

Rebuilt in 1525, it has been divided in recent times into two houses, Nos. 16 and 18. While the façade of No. 18 was modern, that of No. 16, with its window-gratings, retained its ancient aspect. The courtyard was orna-

THE PRINCERIE CLOISTER (*hist. mon.*) BEFORE THE WAR.

mented on two of its sides with two-storied Renaissance galleries (*hist. mon.*). Although of 16th-century construction, the decoration of this cloister was inspired by the Middle Age or Transition Period (*note the crocketted capitals of the pillars and the bases of the latter*).

The house was destroyed by the bombardments, and the cloister is almost entirely in ruins.

THE PRINCERIE CLOISTER IN 1916.

AN OBSERVATION-POST IN MAGDELEINE SQUARE (1916).

The street took its name from a statue of the Virgin on the monumental entrance-gate of the deanery.

Take the Rue de la Magdeleine on the left, beyond the deanery, as far as the **Place de la Magdeleine.**

At No. 2 of this square is an early 16th-century house (sometimes called the "Maison de Jules II."), with a carved triangular pediment supported by two pillars. Built after the decease of Pope Julius II., it was probably erected on the site of the house where he lived while still Cardinal Julian de la Rovère.

At No. 19 *of the square, cross the house in ruins to a kind of garden-terrace at the back,* built on the site of the old ramparts, vestiges of which are still visible. Fine view of the ruins in the Rues Mazel, Châtel and St. Esprit.

Take the Rues Châtel and Belle-Vierge to the **Cathedral** (*see Itinerary, p.* 31).

RUINS IN THE RUE CHÂTEL, SEEN FROM THE CATHEDRAL (1916).

THE CATHEDRAL (*hist. mon.*)

The Cathedral of Verdun, like that of Angers, was one of the first French churches to be dedicated to the Virgin. In the 7th or 8th centuries its patronal festival was The Nativity, but this was changed to The Assumption at the beginning of the 19th century.

It is an ancient edifice, but has often been restored and altered. The original 5th-century church, which it replaced, was built on the ruins of a Roman *castrum*, like those of Rheims, Metz and Trèves.

The Cathedral was consecrated in 1147 by Pope Eugenius III., assisted by eighteen cardinals and St. Bernard. The plans were made by the Rhenish architect Garin, and, contrarily to French practice, included two transepts and two apses. With its four similar spires, two on each choir, it looked, according to a popular saying, like a " bahut " (chest of drawers on legs), turned upside down.

The fire of 1755 caused important alterations to be made which, without suppressing the main lines of the Cathedral, disfigured the interior. These alterations explain the lack of harmony in the edifice.

The four Roman towers with spires disappeared after 1755. Only the two western towers were replaced by the present large ones.

The Cathedral did not greatly suffer from the bombardment of 1916, during the German offensive, but that of April–May, 1917, damaged it very seriously. The vaults were either pierced or brought down, and the roof destroyed. Near the apsis a big shell tore open the ground, bringing to light an unknown subterranean passage or crypt.

VERDUN SEEN FROM ONE OF THE CATHEDRAL TOWERS.

In the foreground : Roof of nave, east transept, and great choir of Cathedral.
In the middle-ground : The Meuse ; on the left, Chaussée Gate ; in the middle, Military Club.
In the background : Line of trees marking the ramparts ; behind, Belleville Village (on the left) and the Pavé Faubourg.
On the horizon : Belleville Hills.

The tourist, arriving at the Place de la Cathédrale, via *the Rue de la Belle-Vierge (see Itinerary, p.* 31), *finds himself in front of the North Façade (photo opposite).*

In the middle is the entrance portal; *on the right,* the Western Transept and the Towers enclosing the remarkable, square-shaped old Choir; *on the left,* the Eastern Transept and polygonal apsis of the Great Choir (*photo below*).

In front of the Towers, on the right of this photograph, is the entrance to Margueritte College, *giving access to the* Bishop's Palace *and the* Cloister (*see pp.* 49–51).

THE CATHEDRAL.

In the middle: The towers around the old choir.
On the left: The North Front and Main Doorway.
On the right: Entrance to Margueritte College, leading to the Bishop's Palace and the Cloister (*see pp.* 49–51).

The Entrance Portal

(*North Front*)

The Gable and Buttresses of the portal are 13th century. Its secular ornamentation replaced, in the 18th century, Gothic statues, which were destroyed as uncouth.

The portal is placed between two chapels; that on the right (16th century) is called "The Chaplet," on account of the chaplets carved on the buttresses.

The Towers

The present bells weigh four and six tons respectively and date from 1756. They were so cast as to have the same proportions and tones as those of the St. Germain-des-Prés Church in Paris.

The Apse of the Great Choir

The basement is the remains of a Roman apse. The upper portion dates from the end of the 14th century.

The bas-reliefs are Roman carvings, re-utilised in the Gothic buttresses. *From right to left* they represent *Adam and Eve;* the *Annunciation* (the Virgin and Angel are separated by a tree, whose shape recalls the Tree of Life on the Chaldean cylinders reproduced on the cloth-stuffs exported from Byzantium);

APSIS OF THE GREAT CHOIR, SEEN FROM THE BANKS OF THE MEUSE (*see p.* 34).

THE GREAT NAVE

In the background: The old choir and organ-loft (the organs had been removed). In the foreground: The marble balustrade of the Great Choir protected by sandbags

Cain and Abel (through an error in perspective, frequently to be found in Egyptian art, the bust and trunk of the two patriarchs are shown in profile, whilst the feet are facing frontwards); an unknown bishop.

The Great Nave and two Choirs

The Great Nave was very seriously damaged by the bombardments. Several bays of the vaulting fell in, leaving bare the timber-work of the roof in ruins.

On entering the Cathedral by the Central Portal in the North Front (see p. 43) the old Choir *(photos, p. 41) is on the right, and the* Great Choir with ciborium *(p. 45) on the left.*

THE GREAT NAVE BEFORE THE WAR

In the background: The Old Choir and the Great Organ. In the foreground: The balustrade of the Great Choir

THE GREAT NAVE SEEN FROM THE OLD CHOIR

In the background: The Great Choir and the Ciborium. The ruined vaults have bared the damaged framework of the roof

The old square choir is intersected by the great organ, as at Albi.

The decoration of the Great Choir dates from 1760. The marble balustrade (*see p.* 44) is a copy of that in the Jardin du Luxembourg, Paris, and replaced the old lateral walls and rood-loft. The gilded canopy, which is a transformation of the antique ciborium of the Gallo-Roman churches, is supported by four twisted columns of grey marble. It is a copy of that of St. Peter's at Rome. Behind it are eighty-six stalls in two superposed rows, and carved panelling (*see p.* 46).

THE CIBORIUM

(The Ciborium was the canopy supported by columns which covered the altars in the early Christian basilicas.

THE STALLS AND WOODWORK OF THE GREAT CHOIR

Stalls and Woodwork of the Great Choir.—Classed as an historical monument in 1905, this Rococo-style woodwork by Lacour of Toul is remarkable for its somewhat secular elegance and fine finish. During the bombardment of Verdun in 1916–1918 it was taken down and put in a place of safety.

THE SHRINE OF ST. SAINTIN

Photographed with the woodwork of the Great Choir at the Exhibition of the Evacuated Art Treasures held in Paris

St. Saintin's Shrine.—This 14th-century shrine contains the relics of the first bishop of Verdun, and is said to represent the ancient church of the Premonstrants of St. Paul.

The South Aisle and Holy Sacrament Chapel

The numerous collateral chapels are 14th, 15th and 16th century. The most interesting is that of the Holy Sacrament. It was finished in 1402, and is Radial-Gothic in style.

In the neighbouring transept there was formerly a "puits" (well), which offended Louis XIV. when he visited the Cathedral in 1687. The Chapter had it filled up and covered with a stone, on which was carved the letter "P."

The Chapel of the Virgin contains an interesting mutilated monument to Archdeacon Wassebourg, carved in the 16th century to perpetuate the true image of Our Lady of Verdun seated and crowned.

MONUMENT TO ARCH-DEACON WASSE-BOURG, CHAPEL OF THE VIRGIN

UPPER PORTION OF DOOR IN OLD ROMAN APSE, REMOVED TO THE VESTRY.

ROMAN CAPITAL OF THE GREAT CRYPT FILLED IN IN 1755, EXCEPT TWO BAYS DECORATED WITH PAINTINGS.

THE LAST JUDGMENT. PAINTING ON THE VAULT OF THE CRYPT.

Enter the courtyard of the Bishop's Palace by the door of the Margueritte College (see p. 43). The Seminary seen in the background of the photo has been completely destroyed since 1916. *The door with steps in front led formerly to a staircase descending to the Cloister. In May,* 1919, *this staircase was easily accessible, in spite of the débris all around.*

COURTYARD OF THE BISHOP'S PALACE AND THE CATHEDRAL IN 1916

The Bishop's Palace

This fine spacious building was erected in 1725–1755 from the plans of *Robert de Cotte.* It has two terraces and a garden, with a view over the whole town. Under the First Empire it was a senatorial palace.

At the time of the separation of the Church from the State it was turned into a **museum.** The latter contains a fine collection of medals and coins, also numerous fragments of the ancient Abbey of St. Vanne, which was inside the Citadel. These fragments include the remains of a Pagan altar, a Corinthian capital with Barbarian ornamentation, and an ivory comb with inscriptions, said to have been given by Emperor St. Henri to the Abbot of St. Vanne in 1024.

THE BISHOP'S PALACE. FAÇADE LOOKING ON THE COURTYARD AND ENTRANCE TO THE MUSEUM.

THE CLOISTER
On the left: Aisle of the Cathedral (*see p.* 47) and the Transept with ruined roof. In the background: The East Gallery of the Cloister

The Cloister (*Hist. Mon.* 13th and 14th centuries)

The door of Margueritte College and the courtyard of the Bishop's Palace lead to the Cloister (see photos, pp. 43 *and* 49).

Although Gothic in structure, parts of the carved decorative work announced the coming Renaissance (helmeted warriors and antique personages crowned with laurels).

Some of the keystones of the vaulting, representing bloated, bearded faces, are said to be caricatures of the canons of the Cathedral, made by the workmen who built the cloister, to revenge themselves for the Church's stinginess.

THE WEST GALLERY IN WHICH THE STAIRCASE LEADING TO THE CLOISTER OPENS OUT (1914)
The arrangement of the blind windows against the walls is very rarely met with

THE CLOISTER SEEN FROM ONE OF THE CATHEDRAL TOWERS

In the background: the East Gallery. On the right the Seminary and South Gallery in ruins. In the town is seen St. Saviour's Church against the green background of the fortifications

The heavy Seminary buildings, erected on two of the galleries, are 19th century. They were almost entirely destroyed by the bombardments.

THE SOUTH GALLERY OF THE CLOISTER BEFORE THE WAR

Its present state is shown in the above photograph

CHÂTEL GATE. BEHIND THE CATHEDRAL.

On leaving the Cathedral, the tourist arrives almost immediately at the small Place Châtel, the highest point of the town. Take the Rue Châtel to the **Châtel Gate.**

From the ancient "Fermeté" rampart, only this machicolated gate (formerly called "Champenoise") is visible near the small "Place Châtel."

On leaving the Châtel Gate, go down the Rue des Hauts Fins to the corner of the Rue Montgaud: Blockhouse for four machine-guns to defend the town.

Cross the Esplanade de la Roche to the **Citadelle.**

THE CITADELLE

From the Esplanade de la Roche, the arrangement of which dates from 1780–1783, there is a fine view of the Meuse valley and the prairies known as **Pré-l'Evêque.**

The entrance to the **Citadelle** opens on the Esplanade de la Roche, while the Citadelle proper occupies the site of the ancient **Abbey** and **Church of St. Vanne,** erected in the Merovingian Period and 15th century on the hill where, in the days of Clovis, the Dragon with poisoned breath was said to live. According to the legend St. Vanne first tamed the dragon, then led it to the River Meuse, where it was drowned.

The first Citadelle was begun in 1552, continued under Henri IV. by Errard, and finished in 1630 under Governor Marillac. The second was the work of Vauban (1670–1682). The church of St. Vanne was included and preserved in both citadelles, but was later pulled down (1831–1835) by order of the Military Authorities. The old Gothic cloister was spared and turned into barracks in 1835. It was destroyed by the German bombardment during

THE CITADEL BUILDINGS AFTER THE BOMBARDMENTS OF 1916

(Photographed in 1917)

THE CITADEL AND ST. VANNE TOWER, WITH WIRELESS ANTENNA.

the siege of 1870. Of the Abbey, only a square Roman Tower of the 11th century remains (*see photo above*).

THE CITADEL RAMPARTS AND NEUVE GATE.

(*Entrance to the town by the* G. C. 34, *continued by the Rue de Rû. See coloured plan between pp.* 30 *and* 31.)

DORMITORY IN THE CASEMATES.

The Citadel during the War

During the late War, the Citadelle was often a target for the German heavy guns, but its deep underground vaults provided secure shelter for the population before the general evacuation, as also for the public services and reinforcements. Most of the regiments which took part in the battles of 1916 passed through the Citadelle.

It was in one of the casemates that the President of France, M. Poincaré, handed to the Municipal Authorities of Verdun, on September 13th, 1916, the decorations conferred on that City by the Chiefs of State of the Allied countries (*see p.* 30).

CO-OPERATIVE CANTEEN IN THE CITADEL.

THE RUE DES GROS-DEGRÉS.

On leaving the Citadelle, turn to the right immediately after the entrance and follow the glacis which passes underneath the terraces of the Bishop's Palace. After a sharp turning near the Manutention, the tourist arrives at the **Rue de RÛ.**

Take the latter as far as the **Rue des Gros-Degrés,** one of the most picturesque streets of Old Verdun, which also suffered greatly from the German bombardment. It is composed of eighty steps, divided into seven unequal flights, with a hand-rail erected in 1595. *The photograph opposite was taken from the bottom of the stairs.*

Take on the right the Rue du Pont des Augustins and cross the curious canal of the same name (*photo below*) to visit the Lower Town, which is crowded with picturesque old streets and narrow bridges over the winding canals.

Return to the **Place Mazel.**

If the tourist has time, he may go from here to the **St. Victor Gate,** *situated at the exit of Verdun, in the direction of Metz, Nancy, Toul, and Commercy* (*see* p. 56, *and plan between pp.* 30 *and* 31).

THE CANAL DES AUGUSTINS.

ST. VICTOR'S GATE

From the Place Mazel to St. Victor's Gate

(*See plan between pp.* 30 *and* 31)

Cross the St. Croix bridge, take the Rue de l'Hôtel-de-Ville, then the Rue St. Sauveur, in which is the **Hospice St. Catherine.**

The **Hospice St. Catherine** was the birthplace of Bishop St. Airy. According to tradition the Bishop, on receiving a visit from Childebert II., caused his last barrel of wine to be brought in. Giving thanks, he was miraculously able to satisfy the deep-drinking Franks for several days. (*This legend is probably connected with the planting of the vineyards in the region of Verdun.*)

Opposite the Church of St. Catherine is the colonaded front of the former **Congrégation Notre-Dame Monastery,** now a school.

Further on are the **Church of St. Victor,** Rustic-Gothic in style, *and the* **Gate** of the same name (*photo above*).

Stairs on the right of St. Victor's Gate lead to the Citadelle Curtain 16, whence there is a fine view of the city.

THE DOORWAY OF THE CONGRÉGATION NOTRE-DAME (63 RUE DE L'HÔTEL-DE-VILLE)

VISIT TO THE BATTLEFIELD

The following Itinerary is divided into two parts :

1. The right bank of the Meuse, including the forts (Tavannes, Souville, Vaux and Douaumont). *See pp.* 57–87.
2. The left bank of the Meuse, including Cumières, Mort-Homme, Hill 304 and Avocourt. *See pp.* 88–111.

1st ITINERARY: THE RIGHT BANK OF THE MEUSE AND THE FORTS

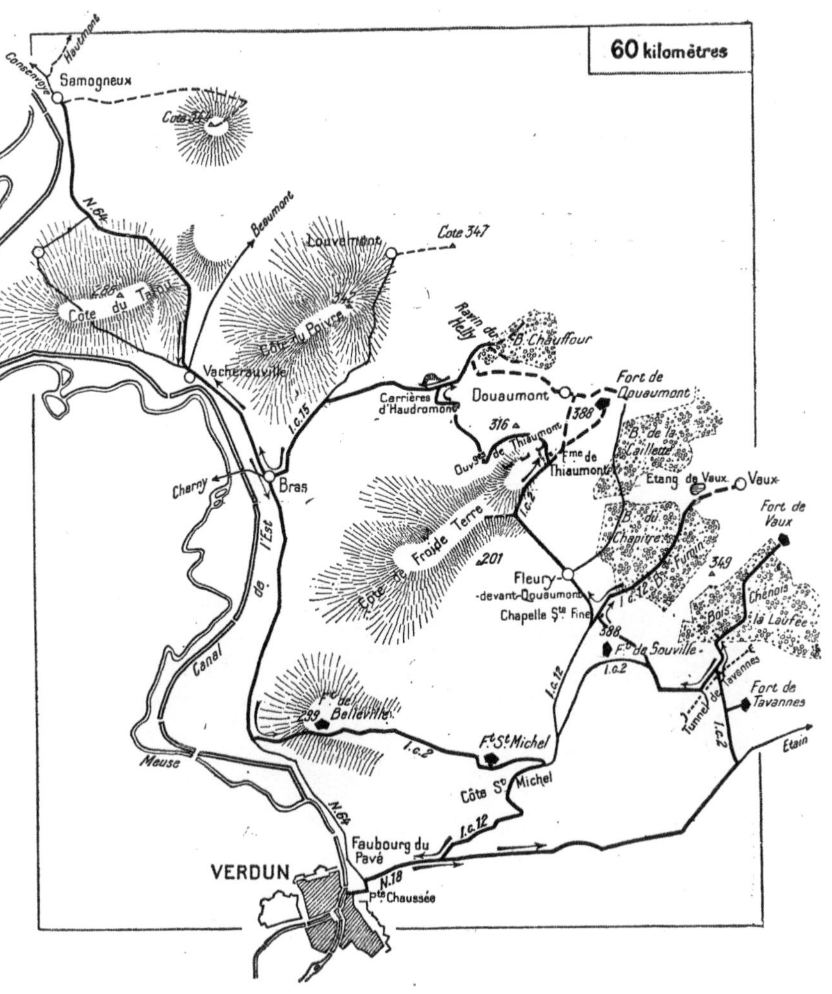

LEAVING VERDUN BY THE CHAUSSÉE GATE (*see p.* 34).

I.—From Verdun to Tavannes Fort

Leave Verdun by the Chaussée Gate, cross the Meuse and the fortified enclosure, and take the Rue d'Etain (R. N. 18) *on the left. Go up the Faubourg Pavé.* This road, used by the relief troops in the Vaux-Douaumont sector, was heavily and continually shelled until Verdun was finally cleared in December, 1916.

MILITARY CEMETERY AT THE EXIT OF THE FAUBOURG PAVÉ.

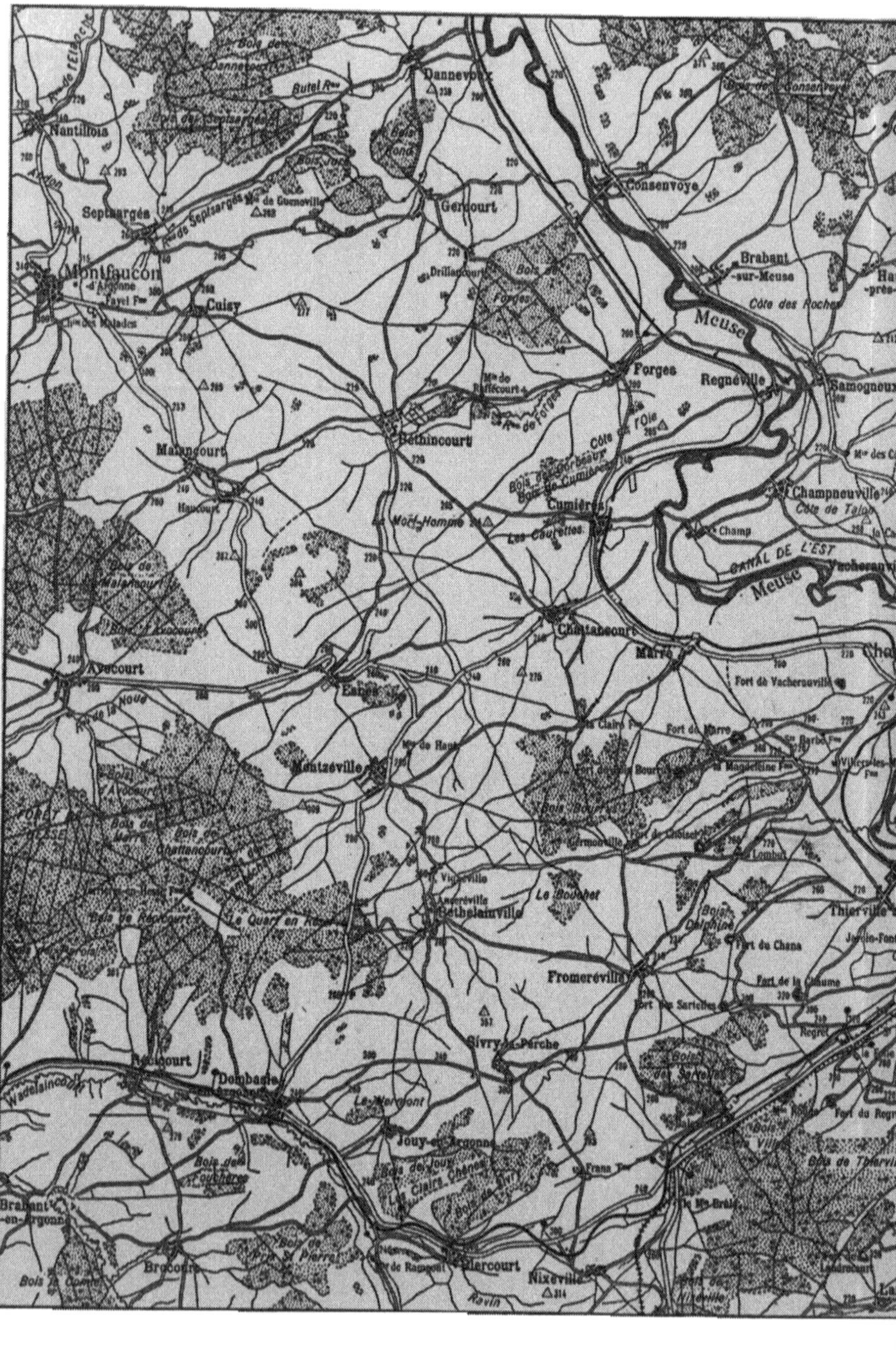

Dannevoux
Nantillois
Butel Fme
Bois Rond
Septsargés
Gercourt
Consenvoye
Montfaucon
d'Argonne
Cuisy
Drillancourt
Bois de Forges
Brabant
-sur-Meuse
Côte des Roches
Meuse
Forges
Regnéville
Béthincourt
Côte de l'Oie
Malancourt
Haucourt
Cumières
Champneuville
Côte de Talou
Le Mort-Homme
Les Caurettes
Champ
CANAL DE L'EST
Meuse
Bois de Malancourt
Chattancourt
Marre
Avocourt
Esnes
Fort de Vacherauville
Fort de Marre
Montzéville
Bois Bourrus
Germonville
Fort de Choisel
Bois de Marre
Le Quart en Réserve
Bois de Récicourt
Le Bouchet
Bethelainville
Fort du Chana
Fort de la Chaume
Fromeréville
Thierville
Sivry-la-Perche
Récicourt
Dombasle
Bois des Sartelles
Fort du Regret
Jouy-en-Argonne
Bois de Thierville
Brabant
-en-Argonne
Brocourt
Blercourt
Nixéville
Ravin

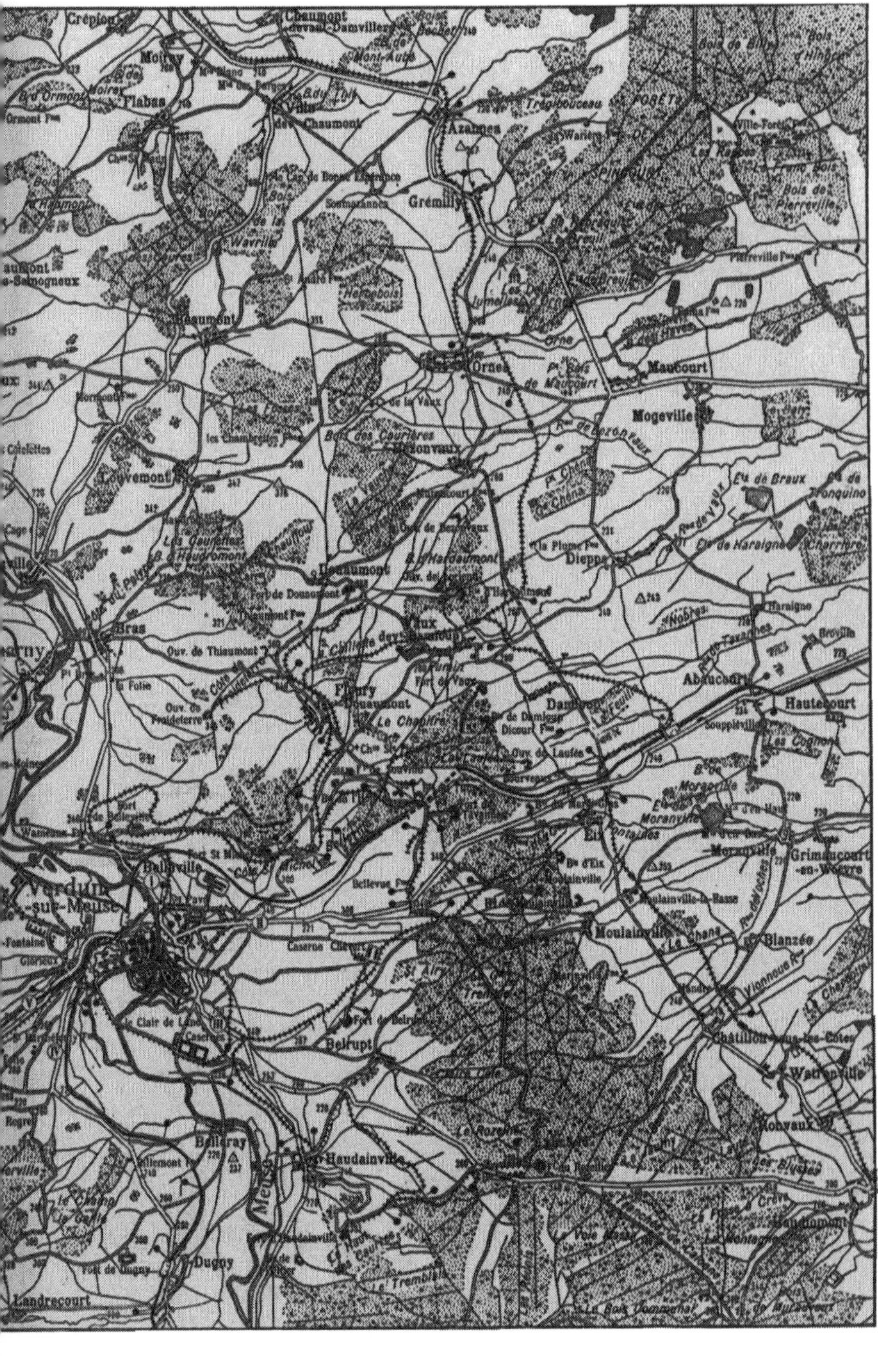
Crépion
Chaumont devant-Damvillers
Moirey
Flabas
Ville devant-Chaumont
Azannes
Gremilly
Beaumont
Herbebois
Ornes
Maucourt
Mogeville
Bezonvaux
Louvemont
Dieppe
Bras
Douaumont
Vaux
Fleury
Damloup
Abaucourt
Hautecourt
Eix
Moranville
Grimaucourt en-Woëvre
Belleville
Verdun sur-Meuse
Moulainville
Blanzée
Belrupt
Châtillon-sous-les-Côtes
Watronville
Ronvaux
Belleray
Haudainville
Haudiomont
Dugny
Landrecourt

THE INTERIOR OF TAVANNES FORT

At the side of the Municipal Cemetery (on the left) is a Military Cemetery containing more than 5,000 graves (*photo, p. 58*).

Follow N. 18 *for about six kilometers, then turn to the left into the road leading to* **Tavannes Fort,** *situated about a kilometer from the main road.*

Tavannes Fort dominates the ground behind the Vaux-Souville line and the Etain-Verdun road. The Germans, in their effort to reach Souville, sought by frequent bombardments to destroy the fort which resisted stubbornly, but on May 7th a 17-inch shell destroyed one of the arches and caused serious damage.

Near the fort, on the Verdun-Etain railway, is the long **Tavannes Tunnel.** Although the entrances were constantly shelled by enemy artillery, it was used as a shelter for the reserves of the Vaux-Souville sector and as a munitions depot. Bunks were fitted up in three superimposed rows, 300 to 450 feet in length, and separated by spaces, where numerous other troops slept as they could on the ground. Despite the ventilating shafts, the air remained foul, owing to the perspiration of the men and the rudimentary sanitary arrangements. To complete the misery of the men, a grenade depot blew up on the night of September 4th, causing many victims.

THE SOUTHERN MOAT OF TAVANNES FORT

THE CAR COMING FROM TAVANNES FORT TAKES THE ROAD ON THE RIGHT TO VAUX FORT. THAT ON THE LEFT LEADS TO SOUVILLE FORT

II.—From Tavannes Fort to Vaux Fort

Return to the road by which the fort was reached (I. C. 2) *and turn into it on the right. About* 300 *yards further on, at the fork* (*see photo above*), *take the right-hand road* (*the other leads to Souville Fort*). On the left is the ravine which precedes the entrance to Tavannes Tunnel. At first the road rises, then dips down to Bourvaux Ravine. (*On the right the road to* Bourvaux Battery *is visible.*) The road zig-zags, then scales Hill 349, leading to Vaux Fort, after crossing through the woods of La Laufée and Chenois, of which only a few broken, branchless trunks remain.

Chenois and Laufée Woods and the Damloup Battery.—Before and after the fall of Vaux Fort, these positions were often attacked by the Germans, especially in June, July and September, 1916.

From June 2nd to 4th the Damloup battery and its approaches, defended by units of the 142nd and 52nd Line Regiments, repulsed sharp German attacks and prevented the enemy from debouching from Damloup. The defence of the battery lasted till July 2nd, the defenders, in constantly diminishing numbers, being attacked and bombarded without intermission. On July 3rd

THE ROAD TO VAUX FORT (*the latter is in the background*).

LAUFÉE WOOD IN 1917

a German attack, preceded by an intense bombardment, resulted in the capture at about 1 p.m. of the greater part of the battery, but the remnant of a French company held its ground in the southern part of the work. At 3 p.m. only fifty men of the company were left; at 8 p.m. twenty, but still they hung on until an hour later they were reinforced by another company, which succeeded in crossing the barrage. At two o'clock next morning the French repulsed the enemy at the point of the bayonet and recaptured the entire battery.

After losing it on July 12th, the French re-took the battery in a bayonet charge on October 24th, while General Lardemelle's division re-captured Chenois Wood (*see p.* 19).

CHENOIS WOOD IN 1917. VAUX FORT IS IN THE BACKGROUND.

VAUX FORT IN 1916 (*photographed from aeroplane*).

Vaux Fort.—Built of masonry about the year 1880, afterwards of concrete, and finally of reinforced concrete, the fort was only completed in 1911. Smaller and less powerful than Douaumont Fort, it dominates the plateau to the south of Vaux Ravine and the reverse side of Douaumont Plateau. Therein lies its importance. On March 9th Germany announced triumphantly to the world that the VIth and XIXth reserve regiments of Posen had "taken by assault the armoured Fort of Vaux, as well as numerous neighbouring fortifications."

This communiqué was untrue. Two battalions of the XIXth regiment of Posen had in reality gained a footing on Vaux Hill on March 9th, but they were mown down at close range by French fire. As a matter of fact, three months of uninterrupted costly effort were necessary before the Gremans were able to enter Vaux Fort.

On March 10th and 11th, in four column formation, they attacked the slopes leading to the fort. Literally mowed down, regiment after regiment

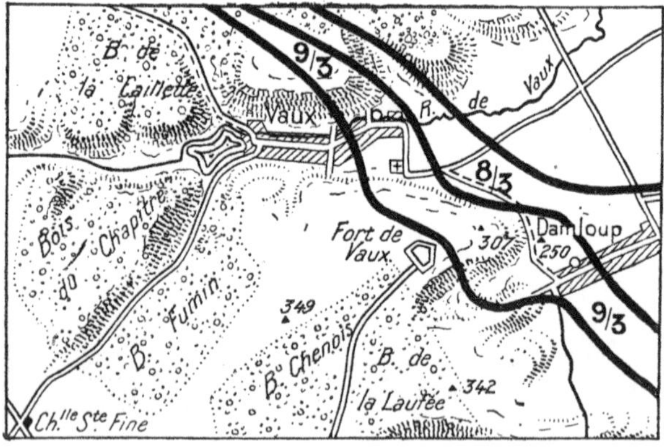

GERMAN ADVANCE ON MARCH 8 AND 9, 1916,

VAUX FORT. THE MOATS IN JUNE, 1916

left heaps of dead and wounded in front of the French wire entanglements; 60 per cent. of the enemy effectives engaged melted away in these two sanguinary days. After a terrific artillery preparation—five times on March 16th and six times on March 18th—they again swarmed up the slopes of the fort only to be thrown back with heavy loss. On April 2nd the enemy sustained another check, but during the night of June 2nd they reached the northern moat. While, on June 4th and 5th, six of their divisions attempted unsuccessfully to outflank the fort on the north by Fumin and on the south by Chenois Wood, the battle continued to rage on the fort itself and in front of the southern side.

From March to June 2nd, the fort and its surroundings received no less than 8,000 large calibre shells daily. Only one entrance was left, *i.e.* the north-west postern, which enemy artillery fire rendered unserviceable. The commander of the fort (Raynal) and his men were imprisoned in the underground chambers of the fort, being no longer able to hold their ground outside. To economise food and water, the surplus contingents were ordered to leave the fort. On the night of the 4th a first detachment made its escape under the direction of Aspirant Buffet, who returned to the fort the next evening with orders. The same night 100 more men managed to get away. Carrier pigeons and optical signals now furnished the only means of communication with the French lines. On the 4th, the last pigeon was released. On the morning of the 5th, thanks to two signalmen who volunteered to change a

THE APPROACHES TO VAUX FORT IN MARCH, 1916

The Fort is on the left at the back

signal post which the Commandant had difficulty in observing, communications were maintained. The same night the Commandant sent his last message that could be read in its entirety, and which ended: "We have reached the limit, officers and soldiers have done their duty. Long live France!" Nevertheless, the fort continued to hold out and refused to surrender. On the night of the 6th reinforcements tried to relieve it and reached the moat of the counter-scarp, but after losing nearly all their officers they were compelled to fall back. The Germans gained a footing in the ruins of the superstructure, and eventually succeeded in driving the French out of the casemates by lowering baskets of grenades with retarded fuses and by using liquid fire and poison gas. Driven back into the underground passages, the French continued the fight with grenades and bayonets. The 2nd regiment of Zouaves and the Colonial regiment of Morocco made a last effort on the morning of the 8th to relieve the garrison. They reached the approaches of the fort, from which clouds of thick black smoke, caused by a violent explosion in one of the casemates, were pouring. Exposed to the fire of the enemy machine-guns installed in the superstructure of the fort and attacked by constantly increasing reinforcements, they were unable to hold their ground.

When, on the night of June 8th, after seven days and nights of continual fighting, the heroic defenders of the fort were at last overpowered, the unwounded among them had not tasted a drop of water for two days.

Five months later (November 2nd) the Germans were driven out of the fort, which they hurriedly evacuated (*see pp.* 63-64).

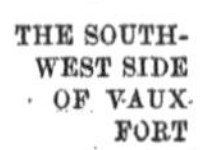

THE SOUTH-WEST SIDE OF VAUX FORT

THE OLD ENTRANCE TO SOUVILLE FORT (Sept. 1916)

III.—From Vaux Fort to Souville Fort

On leaving Vaux Fort return along the same road to the fork (*photo, p.* 60) *and turn to the right. About one kilometer from the fork, on the left, the escarpments of* **Souville Fort** border the road. *Go to the fort on foot* (*about* 200 *yards from the road*).

Souville Fort, which stands as high as that of Douaumont, commands the background of the Douaumont—Vaux line. After taking this line, the enemy, from June 15th to 22nd, undertook the destruction of the fort. On the 23rd the entire CIIIrd German Division attacked, but was repulsed with very heavy losses in front of the French second line trenches. The attack was renewed by two divisions on July 11th and 12th, but failed to reach the moats of the fort.

SOUVILLE FORT (*March* 1917).

PANORAMA SEEN FROM THE CROSS-ROA

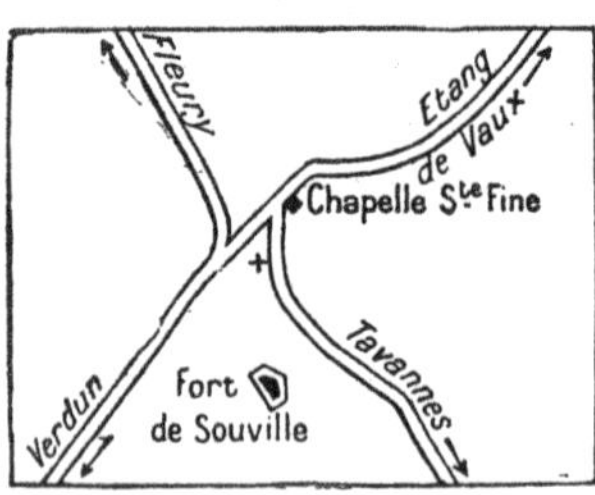

The " + " on the sketch-map opposite shows the spot from where the panorama should be viewed. The car in the photo came from Souville Fort, turning to the right towards Vaux Village.

After visiting the village return to the cross-roads and take the road on the right to Douaumont, seen on the left half of the above panorama (p. 66). *The bombardments have left no trace of St. Fine Chapel.*

IV.—From Souville Fort to Vaux Village and Pond

After visiting Souville Fort return to the cross-ways at St. Fine Chapel, seen the above photo.

ATTACKING WAVES OF INFANTRY CROSSING FUMIN WOOD (Oct. 1916).

T THE CHAPEL OF ST. FINE (*entirely destroyed*).

It was the ruins of this chapel that the enemy reached on July 12th, 1916, and that the 2nd regiment of Zouaves, at the order of General Mangin, recaptured in order to relieve Souville Fort.

At the cross-roads, take the I. C. 12 *on the right to Vaux village. The road dips down into a gorge between the woods of Le Châpitre and Fumin.*

Chapitre and Fumin Woods.—To the west and east of the road leading to Vaux village, these two woods cover the flanks of the plateau which dominates Vaux Ravine and supports Vaux Fort. It was there that the Germans sought to outflank the fort on the west to reach Souville, but they were held in check during May. From June, 1916, these woods were subjected to bombardments of incredible intensity. A powerful German attack on June 23rd failed, but another on July 12th enabled the Germans to get a footing in Fumin Wood. In August and September frequent enemy attacks gave them temporary local gains. On October 24th and 25th, and again at the end of the month, French counter-attacks captured the enemy strongholds and cleared the woods completely.

The defence of the "R" outworks by the 101st line regiment was intimately connected with the attacks on Fumin Wood and Vaux Fort. These outworks were at the foot of the slopes of Fumin Wood, about half-way between the village and fort of Vaux. Bombarded by heavy guns on June 1st and 2nd, it was unsuccessfully attacked by the enemy at 8 p.m. on the evening of the 2nd. Twice on the 3rd and once on the 4th the French, reinforced by a few units, although deprived of water and subjected to machine-gun fire on the flank, repulsed new German attacks. A company of the 298th which, on the night of the 5th, relieved that of the 101st (reduced to 39 men), held out three days more under increasingly difficult conditions, and was only overpowered on the night of the 8th after the capture of the fort of Vaux. These positions were recaptured during the French offensive of October 2nd, 1916. The works known as the "Petit Dépot," "Fulda Boyau," and "Sablière," bristling with machine-guns and scarcely touched by the French artillery preparation, offered a stubborn resistance, and were only captured by the 74th Division in the evening after a whole day of exceedingly hard fighting.

Vaux-les-Damloup.—From March 8th the Germans sought to enter this village from the Woevre. The 1st battalion of their XIXth regiment of Reserves, believing it to be empty, was well-nigh exterminated. On the 10th,

DEFENCE WORKS IN VAUX VILLAGE (*January*, 1916).

after a nine-hour night bombardment with torpedoes, units of the XVth and XVIIIth C.A. attacked the village. Although numbering more than six to one, it was only after four successive attacks that they gained a footing in the ruins of a block of houses behind the church. Soon after they advanced as far as the ruins of the church. Five times they sought to debouch, but were each time literally mowed down by the fire of the French machine-guns and

WHERE VAUX VILLAGE (*entirely destroyed*) STOOD BEFORE THE WAR.
(*Photo, April 26th*, 1917.)

VAUX POND (*March* 1917).

mountain batteries. After two costly checks on March 16th and 18th the Germans again attacked on the evening of the 30th, but it was only three days later and at the cost of very heavy casualties that they were able to take and keep the village.

The road comes to an end at Vaux Pond. The village extended beyond the wooden foot-bridge seen in the photo. No trace of it is left, and the tourist will look in vain for any indication in the desolate waste around him of this erstwhile picturesque and flourishing village. It has literally been wiped out.

Turn the car round 100 yards from the pond, at the place where a narrow-gauge rail-track formerly ran (see photo below).

VAUX POND IS THE EXTREME POINT WHICH CAN BE REACHED BY MOTOR-CARS.

THE SOUTHERN OUTSKIRTS OF FLEURY AFTER THE FRENCH COUNTER-ATTACK OF JUNE 25TH, 1916.

V.—From Vaux Village to Douaumont Fort

After turning the car round at Vaux Pond, return by the same road to the cross-ways at St. Fine Chapel (*see pp.* 66 *and* 67), continue another fifty yards, then take on the right the road to Douaumont.

About 500 yards farther on is the site of what was the village of **Fleury-devant-Douaumont.**

From June 21st to September 30th, 1916, the village was often disputed. After violently bombarding it from June 21st to 23rd, four German Alpine regiments carried it, pushing forward to the south of the Fleury-Vaux railway where the French 75's checked them with very heavy loss. On the 24th–25th the French reoccupied the eastern part of the village. On the 27th two battalions of the French 241st line regiment entered Fleury, but were soon driven out, after which they clung to the southern and western parts. The enemy bombardment of July 9th–10th levelled the village. On the 11th, picked German troops attacked and outflanked it on the south.

FLEURY. THE GRANDE RUE IN JULY, 1916.

French counter-attacks succeeded on the following days in driving the Germans back somewhat, 800 prisoners being taken in ten days. On August 2nd–3rd the village was reoccupied and 1,350 more prisoners taken. It was lost, then partly retaken on August 5th at the point of the bayonet. Two weeks of constant grenade fighting, from hole to hole, by battalions of Alpine Chasseurs from Alsace, carried all that remained of the trenches adjoining the positions "Trois Arbres" and "Montbrison." On August 17th the Moroccan Colonial Regiment finished the conquest of the village with their usual dash.

In the ruins of Fleury, on the right, there is a road which, after passing through Caillette Wood, comes to an end about 400 *yards from* **Douaumont Fort.** *The latter can be reached from here on foot.*

One kilometer after the ruins of Fleury the road divides. Take the right-hand one, the other leads to Bras by the northern slopes of Froide-Terre Hill.

The uphill road follows the ridge, at the end of which is Douaumont Fort, then passes south of **Thiaumont Redoubt.**

Thiaumont Redoubt, S.W. of Douaumont Fort, dominating Froide-Terre

FLEURY IN RUINS, OCTOBER, 1916.

Hill and the Bras road to the W., and the Fleury road to the S., formed the left extremity of the last but one line of resistance which passed in front of Verdun, *via* the village of Fleury and the forts of Souville and Tavannes. For five months (May–September, 1916), which saw some of the hardest fighting in the battle of Verdun, the Germans wore themselves down against this line. Neither the repeated furious attacks, nor poison gas, nor the incredibly intense bombardments could break the resistance of the French, who clung desperately to their positions.

A little further on the road passes the site of **Thiaumont Farm,** *all traces of which were swept away by the battle.*

Thiaumont Farm, captured on June 1st, was reconquered on the 2nd. The enemy occupied the ruins on the 9th, after their big attack of the previous day. On the 12th, 13th, 15th and 17th they sustained four serious checks in front of the defences. Exasperated at the French resistance, they deluged the positions and those of Froide-Terre, on the 21st, with poison gas and more than 100,000 shells. At 6 o'clock on the morning of the 23rd five Bavarian regiments attacked, but although they reached the defences of

THIAUMONT REDOUBT OCCUPIED BY THE FRENCH IN MAY, 1916

The Central Shelter having been pierced by a shell on May 6th, the Redoubt was afterwards only used as an Artillery Observation-Post. The Entrance Trench in the foreground was each day levelled by enemy shells, only to be re-made during the night.

Froide-Terre, they were unable to hold them. However, those of Thiaumont remained in their hands. In a magnificent attack on June 30th, and despite enemy cross-fire, the French 248th line regiment reoccupied Thiaumont at noon, lost it at four o'clock, but recaptured it again the next day and kept it until relieved, in spite of furious German counter-attacks. From July 4th to 9th Thiaumont was retaken and lost four times by the Germans, but a fifth attack enabled them to hold it. Fighting around the defences was continual during the rest of the month. From August 1st to 4th the French 96th line regiment, supported by the 122nd, reconquered Thiaumont and its approaches. From the 4th to the 8th it was defended by the 81st, but on the evening of the 8th, after losing and retaking it, they were driven out by a powerful German attack. Since June 23rd Thiaumont had changed hands sixteen times.

From the middle of August the French command changed their tactics. Abandoning the costly direct attacks, the redoubt was gradually encircled. On October 24th Moroccan Colonial troops, Zouaves and Tirailleurs, in a dashing grenade and bayonet attack, recaptured Douaumont, the Farm and Redoubt of Thiaumont and the Dame and neighbouring ravines.

THIAUMONT REDOUBT IN RUINS OCCUPIED BY THE GERMANS A MONTH LATER

BARBED-WIRE ENTANGLEMENT IN FRONT OF THE FRENCH LINE

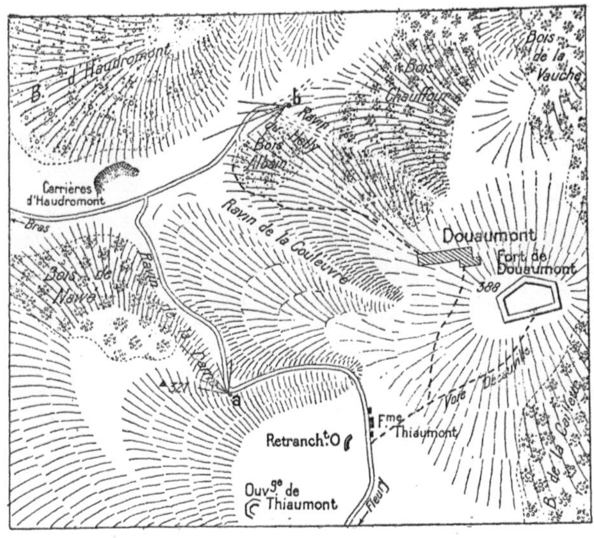

THE APPROACHES TO DOUAUMONT FORT AND VILLAGE.

a — The upper photo on p. 78, **Dame Ravine,** was taken from here.

b — The lower photo on p. 80, **Helly Ravine,** was taken from here.

Leave the car at Thiaumont Farm and go on foot to Douaumont Fort, following the temporary narrow-gauge line for about 1,300 yards. These rails follow the old road which was entirely destroyed.

DOUAUMONT FORT

(*See photo, p.* 29.)

This modern stronghold, which the Crown Prince called "the N.E. angular pillar of the permanent fortifications of Verdun," occupies at Hill 388 the culminating point of the hard limestone plateau which forms the region of Verdun. Lying between Bras Ravine (which descends towards the W. and the Meuse) and Vaux or Bazil Ravine (extending towards the E. and the Woevre), the fort dominates the entire region. As the key of the battlefield it was fiercely disputed.

Before the battle of 1916 it was only bombarded twice by the German artillery. Of the 250 shells fired at it early in November, 1914, 170 reached the mark without, however, causing serious damage. The few 8-inch shells received on March 29th, 1915, did no damage whatever.

On February 25th, 1916, almost at the beginning of the battle, units of the German XXIVth Infantry Regiment (IIIrd Brandenburgers), wearing French Zouave uniforms, surprised and occupied the fort. On the morning of the 26th the French 153rd D.I. (20th C.) counter-attacked fiercely five times, advancing their line beyond the fort and surrounding the enemy on three

DOUAUMONT FORT IN JANUARY 1916.

sides. Thanks, however, to a communicating trench connecting up with their lines, the enemy were able to keep their ground. From the 26th to the 29th they furiously attacked the approaches of the fort without being able to surround it. A redoubt, 200 yards E. of the fort, was alternately lost and recaptured three times on the 26th. From March 8th to May 19th the fighting continued with varying fortune.

From the 19th to the 22nd French heavy guns bombarded the fort, the explosion of a shell on the 20th causing hundreds of victims. To hamper the enemy Intelligence Service six of their observation balloons were destroyed by a French flying squadron on the morning of the 22nd. At 11.50 the

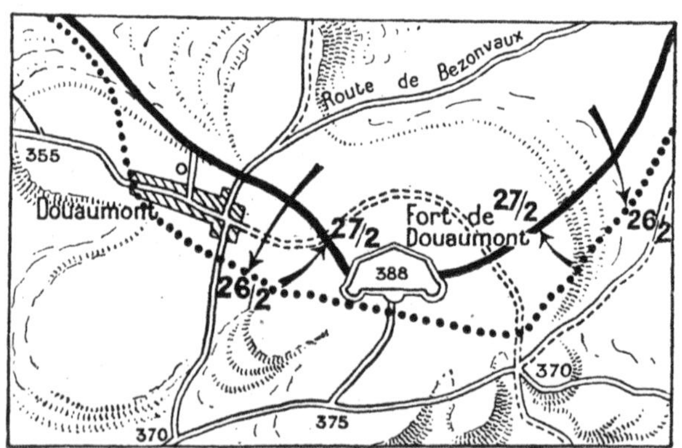

THE FRONT ON THE MORNING OF FEBRUARY 26TH (26/2), AFTER THE GERMANS HAD OCCUPIED THE FORT BY SURPRISE, AND ON THE MORNING OF THE 27TH (27/2), AFTER THE FRENCH COUNTER-ATTACK.

THE ENTRANCE TO DOUAUMONT FORT IN JANUARY, 1916.

10th Brigade (5th D.I.) attacked the fort and its approaches. At noon the 129th line regiment occupied the N. and N.W. corners of the fort. The 74th regiment was unable to take the N.E. corner, but the 36th succeeded in capturing all the trenches west of the Fort. During the night and all the next day the enemy intensified their bombardment and increased the number of their counter-attacks, without breaking through the defences of the 10th Brigade, which maintained all its gains until relieved on the night of the 23rd. Exasperated at this check, the Germans, on the 24th, engaged no less than an army corps of reinforcements and retook the fort.

Five months later (October 24th) they lost it again after a heavy bombardment and attack, during which a French 16-inch shell pierced the superstructure of the fort and started a fire. A dense fog overhung the fort when, at 11.40 a.m., the signal for the attack, directed by General Mangin, was given. When, at about 2.30 p.m. the fog lifted, French observers perceived the Moroccan

THE INTERIOR OF THE FORT ON MAY 22ND, 1916,
THREE HOURS AFTER THE ATTACK.

French Infantry and Sappers in a trench hurriedly made around an outwork of masonry still held by the enemy with machine-guns.

SOLDIERS OF THE MORROCAN COLONIAL REGT. OCCUPYING THE MOATS OF THE RECONQUERED FORT (photographed on the morning of Oct. 25th, 1916. the day after the victory)

Colonials of the Nicolaï battalion scaling the ruins of the fort. On arriving there, the latter found units of the 321st line regiment which, operating *in liaison* on their right, had preceded them and already hoisted the French flag on the ruins of the fort. Two sappers of the 19-2 Co. of Engineers slipped into the basement of the fort, and with the aid of four Colonials captured twenty-four German soldiers, four officers, two guns and three machine-guns in one of the counter-scarp shelters. Other enemy soldiers in one of the casemates surrendered, with the German commander of the fort, on the night of the 24th. The next morning the entire fort, together with a great quantity of arms, munitions and foodstuffs, was in the hands of the French. Four enemy counter-attacks on the 26th failed to retake it.

On the night of the 24th a sergeant of the 4th Zouaves captured, unaided, a German company and six officers. Returning from revictualling duty, he was taken prisoner by some Germans occupying a shelter near the fort Coolly informing them that Douaumont and Damloup Battery had fallen, he called on them to surrender. The attitude of the sergeant was so convincing that after some hesitation they laid down their arms and were brought into the French lines.

Douaumont was entirely cleared on December 15th by the 37th D.I., which fought a hard battle in the woods before the village. Having learned the time of the attack, the Germans were on their guard, but after a furious combat the 2nd Tirailleurs drove back the VIth Prussian Grenadiers and crossed Helly Ravine (*photo, p.* 80).

Hardaumont and **Caillette Woods** and **Douaumont Village** *may be visited on foot from the fort of Douaumont.*

The plateau E. and S.E. of Douaumont Fort ends in wooded slopes, which overhang Vaux (Basil) Ravine. That furthest to the E. contains Hardaumont Wood, while on the most western slope is Caillette Wood. The Germans who, on March 8th and 9th, had taken Hardaumont Redoubt, only entered Caillette Wood on April 2nd, after four days' attacks with asphyxiating gas and liquid fire. Despite a night march of eleven miles, the

74th line regiment (5th D.I.) attacked the enemy vigorously on the morning of April 3rd. On April 3rd, 4th and 5th the French retook the wood, bit by bit. On the 15th three battalions of the 36th line regiment and units of the 120th threw back the enemy between Caillette and Fausse-Côte ravines, while on the 19th the 81st Brigade enlarged these gains. From the 24th to the 26th the Germans tried in vain to advance. On June 1st they engaged two and a half divisions before they were able to occupy the greater part of Caillette Wood. Moreover, their success was only temporary, for on October 24th the French Division of General Passaga ("La Gauloise") drove them definitely out of Caillette Wood and partly from that of Hardaumont. Nearly two enemy divisions were put out of action and seventeen field guns, twenty-five heavy guns, including two of long range, and numerous trench mortars were captured. The reconquest of Hardaumont Wood was completed on December 15th by the same division which captured "Lorient" and Hardaumont Redoubts.

Douaumont Village, situated below and 500 yards to the W. of the fort, was almost encircled on the evening of February 25th, but Zouaves and

RUINS OF DOUAUMONT VILLAGE AND CHURCH.

Tirailleurs extricated it. From the 25th to the 28th the Vth German D.I. made five furious attacks, but were unable to break down the resistance of the 95th line regiment and units of the 153rd D.I. which were defending the village. On March 2nd, after a preliminary bombardment which destroyed the village and isolated the battalion holding it, the CXIIIth German D.I., wearing French helmets, attacked at 1.15 p.m. on the N. and E. The French machine-gunners soon discovered the trick, however, and mowed them down. After a second bombardment the enemy again attacked, overwhelming the defenders, one company of whom resisted to the last man.

The remains of the French battalion took their stand fifty yards S.W. of the village and prevented the enemy from debouching. On the 3rd two battalions of the 172nd and 174th line regiments retook the village at the point of the bayonet. During the night the Germans counter-attacked twice unsuccessfully with heavy loss, 800 dead being counted in front of one of the French trenches. On the 4th a third and more powerful counter-attack succeeded in driving the French from the village, but broke down against new positions 200 yards to the south. The French were compelled to fall back in May and June, but returned victorious to the ruined village on October 24th.

DAME RAVINE.

The road from Thiaumont to Bras follows it, ending at Haudromont Quarries (*see Itinerary, p.* 57). The tree-stumps in the foreground formed part of Chauffour Wood.

POSITION OF GERMAN BATTERY DESTROYED IN CHAUFFOUR WOOD.

HAUDROMONT QUARRIES IN SEPTEMBER, 1917.

VI.—From Douaumont Fort to Bras and Samogneux

A down-hill road leads direct from Douaumont Village to Thiaumont Farm, where the tourist will take his car again.

Follow the road, which turns to the left and passes through Dame Ravine. On all sides the chaotic waste testifies to the terrible hammering which this region received from the guns (*see photo, p.* 78, *and map, p.* 73).

The tourist leaves **Chauffour Wood** *on his right* (*photos*, p. 78).

This wood extends to the north of the road and approaches to within a few hundred yards of Douaumont on the west. The CVth German Infantry was cut to pieces here on the morning of February 26th, 1916, and on March 2nd the XXIst German Division suffered a similar fate there. During a powerful attack around Douaumont on April 16th the Germans occupied a small salient S. of the wood, but were soon after partially driven out, while on December 17th the wood was entirely cleared of them by the Zouaves and Tirailleurs of the 38th D.I. The enemy's efforts to re-take it and Albain Wood to the S.W. were unsuccessful.

Continue to descend; **Haudromont Quarries** *will be reached shortly afterwards.*

Around these positions, which dominate the ravine debouching at the stream near Bras, furious indecisive fighting took place, more especially on March 18th, April 22nd and May 8th, 9th, 10th, 22nd, 26th and 27th, 1916. They were finally taken on October 24th by the French 11th line regiment.

Fighting was very bitter around the quarries, which form a rough oblong 200 to 300 yards long, fifty to sixty yards wide, visible from afar on account of their white colour. The enemy had cut galleries, casemates and shelters in the chalky soil, the whole forming a redoubtable position. After encircling the quarries, the French captured them with grenades.

HAUDROMONT WOOD IN MARCH, 1917

At the bottom of the hill, opposite and below **Haudromont Quarries,** *tourists desirous of visiting* **Helly Ravine** (*see photo below, and map, p.* 73), which was the scene of terrible fighting during the offensive of December, 1916 (*pp.* 20-21), *should turn to the right for about* 300 *yards.*

Return to the starting-point and continue straight along the **Bras Road.**

On the right the tourist comes to the uphill road to **Louvemont,** *which crosses the southern slopes of Poivre Hill. This road is impracticable for carriages beyond Louvemont.*

HELLY RAVINE (*photographed in May,* 1919).

ROAD FROM LOUVEMONT TO ORNES

(Farthest point accessible to motor-cars in May, 1919)

Louvemont and Poivre Hill

At 2.20 p.m. on February 24th, strong enemy forces debouched between **Louvemont** and **Hill 347.** During the night the first French reinforcements, belonging to the 20th C.A., repulsed them. On the 25th, the enemy, in dense formation, outflanked the village on the W. and E. They were checked several times by units of the 37th D.I. and artillery fire, but succeeded in entering the village at 3 p.m., after having practically levelled it by shell fire.

LOUVEMONT VILLAGE IN APRIL, 1917.

FROIDE-TERRE REDOUBT IN 1915

Zouaves, who were still clinging to the outskirts, ran short of ammunition, but on being reinforced by a battalion of Tirailleurs with 50,000 cartridges, continued with the latter to defend the S.E. approaches of the village until the morrow.

Owing to their heavy losses, the French 37th D.I. was compelled to fall back, but the fire from a hundred 75 mm. guns concentrated at Froide-Terre held the Germans in check and prevented their debouching from the village. The French 39th D.I. promptly took up positions in front of the 37th, between Poivre Hill and the Meuse, and barred the road to Bras. Louvemont and its approaches were brilliantly retaken during the French offensive of December 15th, 1916. While a brigade of the 126th D.I. captured Hill 342 in several rushes, the 4th Moroccan Brigade of the 38th D.I., in a running attack, carried the first and second enemy lines, Louvemont and Hill 347, as well as a fortified cavern known as the camp du Henrias, before which one of the victors of Douaumont, Major Nicolaï, was killed.

On August 20th, 1917, four successive lines of trenches were taken by the French 165th D.I., in an attack to the north of Louvemont.

On leaving Louvemont, return by the same way to the Bras Road and take it on the right. Bras village is reached shortly afterwards, where the Itinerary follows the Meuse Valley and N. 64.

Bras.—The Prussians camped here in 1792, during the occupation of Verdun.

THE LAST TRAIN TO PASS AT THE FOOT OF POIVRE HILL IN 1916. IT WAS WRECKED BY ENEMY ARTILLERY

BRAS VILLAGE AND POIVRE HILL IN SEPT., 1917

In 1916 the Germans could not capture it, although they took Poivre Hill which dominates the village to the N.

After several checks (*e.g.* February 25th and March 9th) they occupied Poivre Hill and Vacherauville, but were unable to dislodge the French from the woods to the S.E.

From March, they organised a network of barbed-wire entanglements, concrete galleries, redoubts, shelters, etc., on the hill, converting it into a kind of fortress, but on December 15th the village and hill were rushed by the 112th line regiment in three-column formation, covered on the left by a fourth column and supported by auto-cannon. Veritable bastion, overlooking the Beaumont road and flanking the entire German line, the village could only be captured by surprise, and the latter was complete. German officers were taken in their shelters while dressing. The attack had not been expected before noon or later than 2 p.m. The village was conquered in ten minutes, and Poivre Hill in seven minutes, in a single rush.

From Bras continue northwards to Vacherauville and Samogneux, where the first German attacks at the beginning of the battle of Verdun took place, (*see Itinerary p.* 57.)

RUINS OF BRAS CHURCH, WHOSE TOWER COLLAPSED
(*Photographed in April*, 1917)

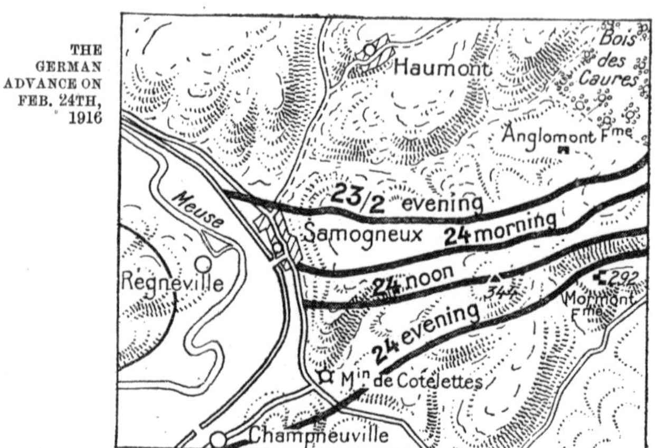

THE GERMAN ADVANCE ON FEB. 24TH, 1916

Vacherauville, entirely destroyed, *is reached soon afterwards. Leave on the right the road to Beaumont and take, a little further on, that leading to Champneuville, which brings the tourist to the top of* **Talou Hill,** *from where the panoramic view on pp.* 86 *and* 87 *was taken.*

Situated in a long bend of the Meuse, **Talou Hill** gradually slopes down to the water's edge. On February 25th the enemy reached this hill which, caught between the fire from both banks, became equally untenable for the French and Germans, and from February 27th was considered as a neutral zone. It was retaken by the French in their offensive of August 20th, 1917, at the same time as the villages of Neuville, Champneuville and Champ.

Samogneux *may be reached from Talou Hill, either by continuing, via Champneuville* (*see outline map, p.* 87), *or by returning to the* R. N. 64.

Subjected to an infernal shell-fire on February 22nd and 23rd **Samogneux** had to be abandoned by the French on the evening of the latter date. It was retaken by the 126th D I. on August 21st, during the French offensive

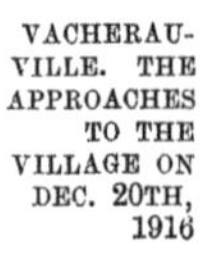
VACHERAUVILLE. THE APPROACHES TO THE VILLAGE ON DEC. 20TH, 1916

THE CENTRE OF SAMOGNEUX VILLAGE ON THE N. 46, IN MAY, 1919.
The village was entirely levelled.

of August, 1917, *i.e.* two days in advance of the scheduled date (*see p.* 23).

SAMOGNEUX CHURCH IN AUG., 1915.

E. of Samogneux and dominating the road from Vacherauville to Beaumont rises **Hill 344,** which, together with Samogneux and Beaumont, fell into the hands of the enemy in 1916. It was retaken during the French offensive of August 20th, 1917, by regiments belonging to the 123rd and 126th D.I. These were almost immediately relieved by the 14th D.I., which for three weeks withstood violent enemy counter-attacks without flinching. On September 9th, in particular, it repulsed an attack by several German divisions which had orders to retake Hill 344 at all costs.

Return to Bras by the same road

VII.—From Bras to Verdun

From Bras take N 64 *towards* **Verdun.** *The road winds across the western slopes of* **Belleville Fort.** *At the top of the hill, take the road on the left (leaving the down-hill road to Verdun).*

The road (IC 2) *passes by* **Belleville Fort** *and along the top of the hill, which formed the last permanent line of resistance, from N.E. of Verdun to* **St. Michel Fort.**

From **St. Michel Fort** *there is a fine run down* **St. Michel Hill,** *to Verdun, which enter by the* **Rue d'Elain** *and* **Chaussée Gate.**

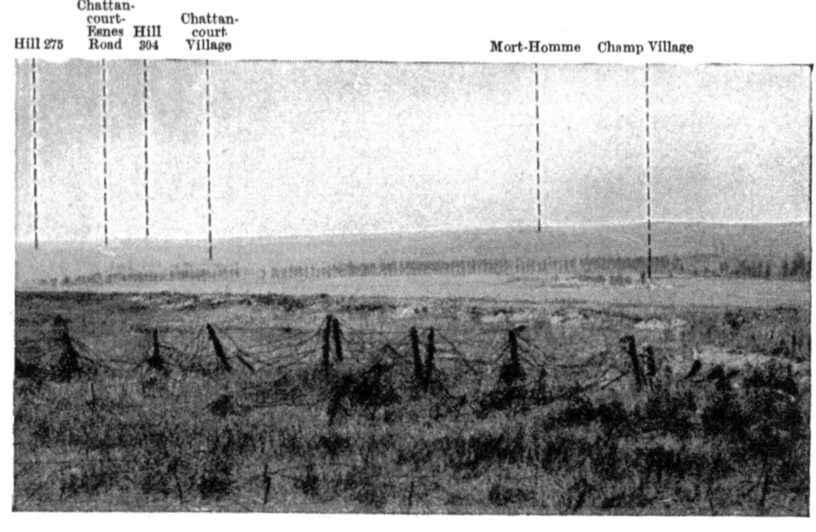

PANORAMIC VIEW OF THE MEUSE VALLEY

(Consider the four parts from left to right, across both pages; the top half fits on to the left of the bottom half.)

From this spot on the road from Vacherauville to Champneuville (see outline map, p. 87), there is a general view of the lines from which the German Offensive started, and of the battlefield on the left bank of the river.

SEEN FROM THE TOP OF TALOU HILL.

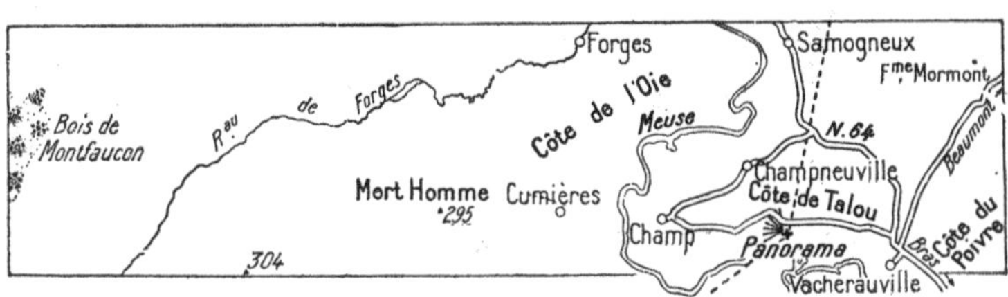

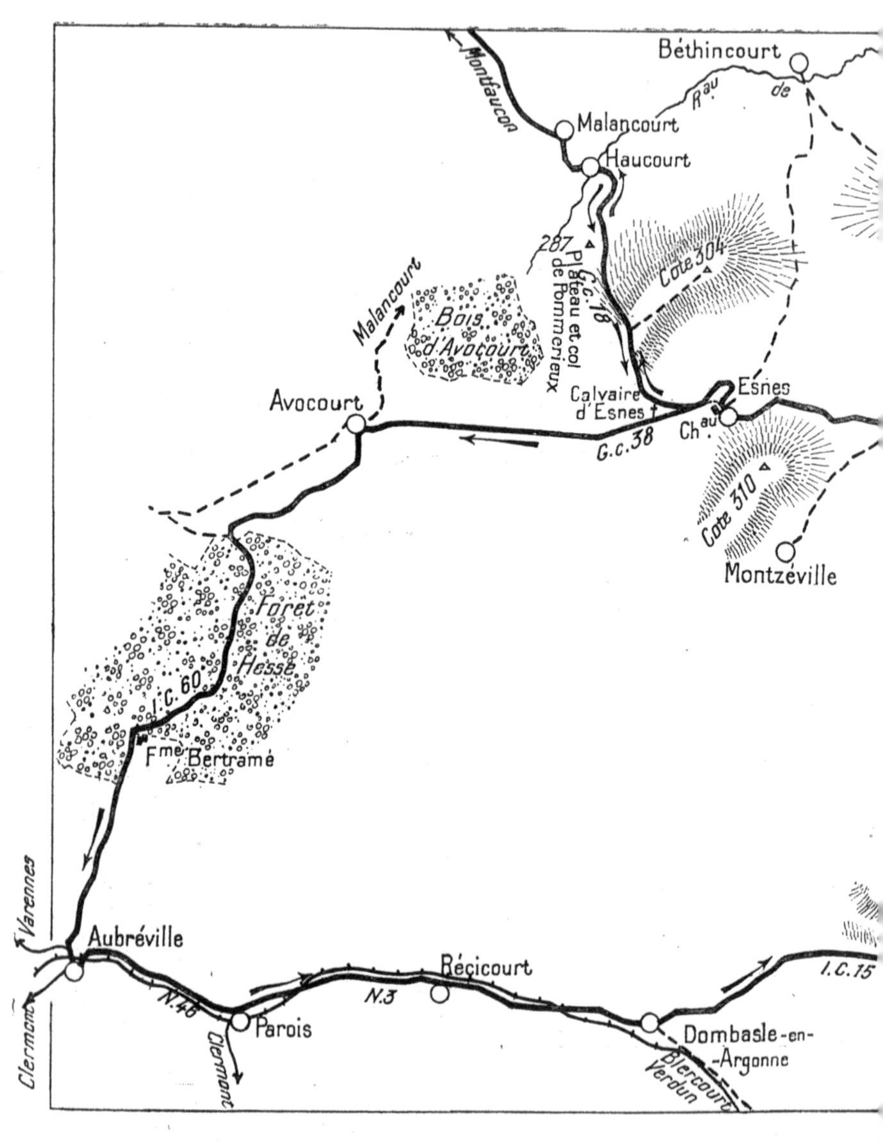

2nd ITINERARY: THE LEFT

including Cumières, Oie Hill, Mort-Homme,

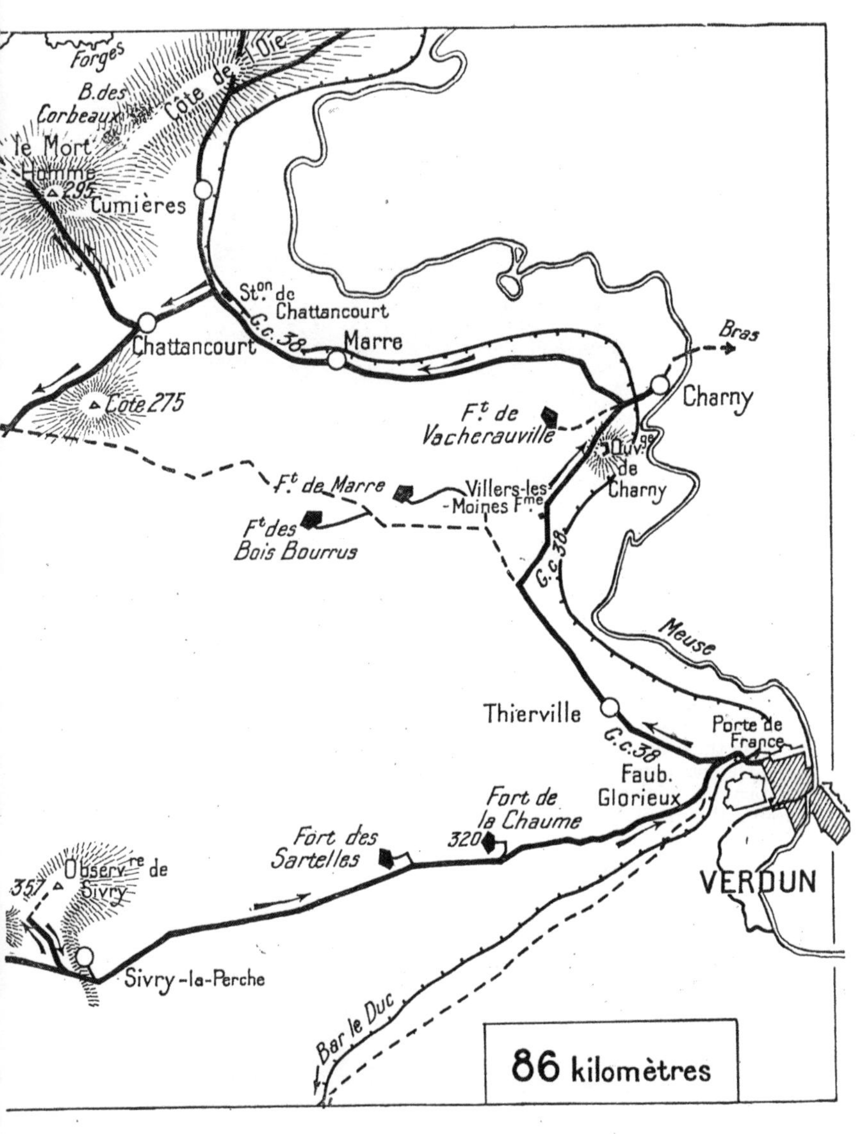

BANK OF THE MEUSE

Montfaucon, Hill 304, and Avocourt (*see description, pp.* 90–111)

THE CHURCH AND MAIN STREET OF CHARNY IN JANUARY, 1916

I.—From Verdun to Charny

Leave Verdun by the Porte de France ; after the railway bridge go straight along G. C. 38 (*see plan between pp.* 30–31). *Cross the Faubourg de Jardin-Fontaine, then Thierville village. Facing it is* MARRE FORT. *At the foot of the hill on which the fort stands, turn to the right. Leaving on the left the ruined* farm of Willers-les-Moines, *the road climbs up the small* Hill 243, *below which is the* strongly fortified **Charny Redoubt.**

On the other side of the level-crossing is **Charny.** It was at Charny that the Germans crossed the Meuse in 1870. Incidentally, they shot the former notary, M. Violard, under the pretext that he had aided an attack by the francs-tireurs of Verdun. In 1916, the village was frequently bombarded by the enemy, particularly on March 31st.

THE CHURCH AND MAIN STREET OF CHARNY SEEN FROM THE OTHER SIDE IN MAY, 1919

On the horizon : Poivre Hill

MARRE VILLAGE IN RUINS.
Beyond the Church take the road on the right to Cumières. That on the left, leading to Bourrus Woods, is impracticable for cars.

II.—From Charny to Cumières

Return to the level crossing, then turn to the right on leaving Charny. The road skirts the northern slopes of the hills on which stands the modern forts of **Vacherauvile, Marre** and **Bourrus Woods.**

Cross through Marre village, in ruins. Beyond the ruined church follow the right-hand road (photo above) to **Cumières.** *Half-way between Marre and Cumières are (on the right) the station of* **Chattancourt,** *(on the left) the road leading to that village.*

Attacked on March 14th and destroyed by shell-fire on April 25th. **Cumières** was only captured by the Germans on the night of May 23rd. Three days later the French retook the eastern portion after a desperate combat. On

CUMIÈRES IN MAY, 1916

PANORAMIC VIEW OF THE RIGHT BANK OF THE MEUSE

May 29th and 30th, after two days of continual bombardment, they were momentarily driven back towards Chattancourt, but a vigorous counter-attack brought them back to the southern outskirts of the village. Caurettes Wood, to the S.W. of Cumières, remained, however, in the enemy's hands.

On August 20th, 1917, Cumières village and wood were retaken by a regiment of the Légion Étrangère, who attacked singing the famous popular song "La Madelon."

CUMIÈRES IN AUGUST, 1917.

SEEN FROM OIE HILL (*see* Outline Map below).

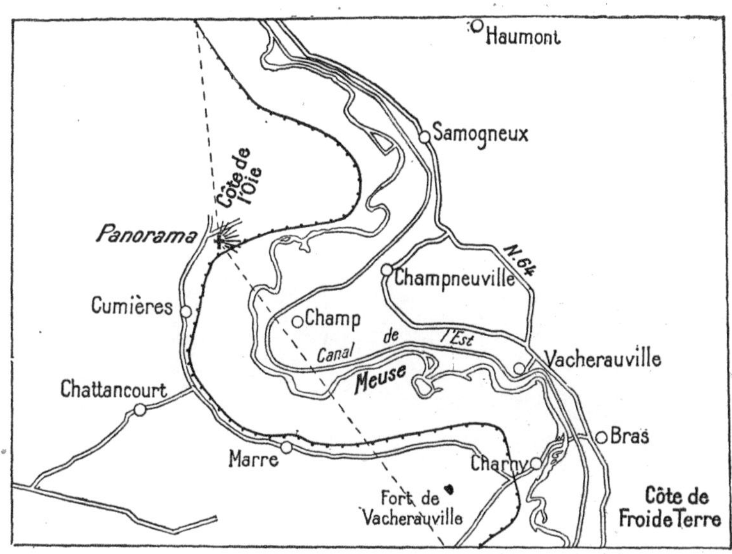

From **Cumières** *continue straight ahead to Oie Hill, from where the above panoramic view was taken.*

CHATTANCOURT ON MAY 16TH, 1916.
On the horizon: The slopes of Mort-Homme.

III.—From Cumières to Chattancourt and Mort-Homme

On leaving Cumières return to the Station of Chattancourt, and take on the right the road to **Chattancourt,** which is about 800 yards further on. This village was completely levelled (*photo below*).

CHATTANCOURT IN 1919.
Nothing remains of the houses and trees. The road seen in the above photo leads to Mort-Homme.

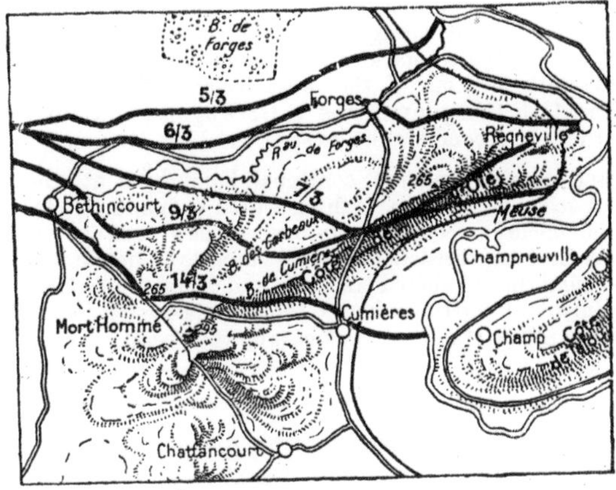

THE GERMAN ATTACKS OF MARCH 5TH–14TH, 1916, ON THE LEFT BANK OF THE MEUSE

From Chattancourt the positions of **Mort-Homme** *may be visited by the road to Béthincourt (the lower photograph on p. 94 shows the beginning of this road).*

Motor-cars can go as far as the top of **Hill 295** *or* **Mort-Homme,** *where it is necessary to turn the car round and return to Chattancourt, as the road is cut near Béthincourt by the Forges stream, which has entirely flooded the lower part of the village.*

Mort-Homme.—Like Hill 304, Mort-Homme was one of the most fiercely disputed positions on the left bank. It consists of twin hills: No. 265 (of which the Béthincourt—Cumières road skirts the summit) and No. 295 (the Mort-Homme proper, round which the road winds on the N.E.), and formed an excellent observation-post and artillery position in front of the real line of resistance.

On March 5th, 1916, the German offensive, which, until then, had been confined to the right bank of the river, developed with great violence on the left flank, progressing in six days to the slopes of Mort-Homme.

On the 14th, after a five-hours bombardment with shells of every kind and size, sometimes at the rate of 120 a minute, the enemy's Infantry attack on Mort-Homme began. The Germans took and kept Hill 265, but the French Infantry and Zouaves, after a magnificent defence, held their ground on Hill 295—the key to the entire position—and in night counter-attacks drove back the assailants to the N.W. counter-slopes.

From March 15th to the end of December, 1916, the Germans launched at least fifteen particularly violent attacks against Hill 295, sacrificing countless men and huge quantities of munitions. On March 16th, 17th and 31st, and April 9th and 10th, French Chasseurs and Infantry repulsed the enemy in terrible hand-to-hand fighting. On April 22nd, 23rd and 24th the French 40th D.I., by its resistance and brilliant counter-attacks, broke up as many as three enemy attacks in one day, and re-established the French front as it was on April 5th. Further German attacks on Hill 295 followed on May 7th, 20th and 22nd, June 29th, July 12th and December 28th. Their furious offensive of May 20th alone brought them momentarily on the S.W. crest of Hill 295 and as far as the French second-line trenches, which were retaken on June 15th.

At that time the sector of Mort-Homme and Hill 304 was commanded by General de Maud'huy, whose courage and coolness are legendary in the army. The exploits of the French troops at Mort-Homme during the difficult period of 1916 were countless. One of the most brilliant was accomplished on April 9th by the 11th Company of the 151st Regiment of Infantry, which had received orders to reconquer the crest of the Mort-Homme.

Laughing and singing under a continual bombardment, this company went into line, a section at a time, with measured step and rifle in hand. On approaching the enemy trenches, the men rushed forward under heavy machine-gun fire and captured a large and important network of trenches. Promptly organising the conquered trenches, and despite an extremely intense enemy bombardment of thirty-six hours, the men succeeded in re-establishing the *liaison* with the 8th Battalion of Chasseurs on their right, making it possible

THE SOUTH-WESTERN SLOPES OF MORT-HOMME IN JANUARY, 1917.

to reform the line which had been broken, and which the enemy afterwards tried in vain to pierce, until May 20th.

In 1917 the sector was often the scene of violent combats, especially on January 25th, and March 18th, 20th and 29th. After many efforts and at heavy cost the Germans succeeded in occupying Hill 265 and the crest of Hill 295, where they organised formidable defences, including deep shell-proof tunnels.

On August 20th, 1917, during the French attack along the entire Verdun front, the 31st D.I. carried all the German defences and recaptured the Mort-Homme and its tunnels, including the one known as the **"Crown-Prince,"** which was "cleaned out" by the Foreign Legion. In one of the tunnels several cavalry-men, units of the XXXVIth and a whole battalion of the XXth Regiment of the German Reserve, were captured, while among the officers taken

MORT-HOMME AFTER THE ATTACK OF AUGUST, 1917 (see p. 23).

was Count Bernstorff, nephew of the ex-German Ambassador to the United States. An entire staff was captured in another of the tunnels.

Corbeaux Wood.—The plateaux dominated by the two Mort-Homme Hills are cut into on the north of the high road by a ravine bordered by Corbeaux Wood. This wood offers favourable cover for the massing of attacking troops. It was by this fiercely disputed route that the enemy tried to reach Hill 295. On March 6th the French line was brought back in front of the wood. On the 7th the enemy, after bombarding it, succeeded in getting a footing there, but on the following day the 92nd Infantry Regiment, in a magnificent counter-attack, retook the wood in twenty minutes. On the morning of the 10th, reinforced by another infantry battalion, the same regiment further captured the N.E. outskirts of Cumières Wood (to the E. of Corbeaux Wood), but in the evening, deprived of its commanding officer (Colonel Macker, who had fallen that morning), and lacking the support of the French artillery, which the trees prevented from seeing the rocket-signals, the regiment was compelled to fall back before an impetuous attack by a whole enemy division. However, it was only at frightful cost that the Germans were able to score these two successes, as the French gave ground only inch by inch.

The wood was retaken by the Foreign Legion Regiment on August 20th, 1917 (*see p.* 23).

MORT-HOMME
Trenches captured in August, 1917

THE ROAD FROM CHATTANCOURT TO ESNES, AT THE FOOT OF HILL 275.

In the background the road forks, that on the left going to Montzéville, the one on the right to Esnes. The tourist should take the latter.

IV.—From Mort-Homme to Esnes.

From Mort-Homme return to the starting-point at Chattancourt, and take on the right the road to Esnes (see photo at the bottom of p. 94).

This fairly steep road scales the northern slopes of Hill 275. Driving is

ESNES VILLAGE IN 1919.

On the left, THE CASTLE; *on the right,* THE CHURCH.

ESNES IN JANUARY, 1916

rather difficult by reason of the numerous shell holes in the road. A pass is soon reached, from which Hill 304 can be seen opposite (*photo, p.* 98).

This road crosses all the organisations of the first line shelters, posts of commandment, dressing-stations, etc. *Continue as far as a crossing* (visible in *photo, p.* 98), *where turn to the right into* **Esnes.**

By reason of its position, S. of Hills 304 and 295, Esnes was an important base of operations during the Battle of Verdun. It was subjected to frequent enemy bombardments, of which the most violent occurred on March 20th and 21st, April 5th, 6th, 12th, 25th and 26th, and June 22nd, 1916.

The three photographs on pp. 98 and 99 show the aspects of the village at three different stages of the battle.

ESNES ON SEPTEMBER 25TH, 1916.

FROM MORT-HOMME TO BOURRUS WOODS: PANORAMIC VIE

V.—From Esnes to Montfaucon, via Hill 304

After passing in front of the ruins of Esnes Church, continue straight ahead, taking the second road on the right (not the first, which leads to Béthincourt—see photograph above).

The road on the left ends in a very steep rough track and is impracticable for cars.

The road to be followed zig-zags up to the **Wayside Cross of Esnes,** *from which there is a magnificent view of the battlefields on the left bank from Mort-Homme to Bourrus Woods (Panorama above).*

At the Wayside Cross take the road to the right.

The left-hand one (seen in the foreground on photo, p. 101) *leads to Avocourt. The tourist will take it on his return from* **Montfaucon.**

The one on the right (in the foreground on photo, p. 100) *passes between* **Hills 287 and 304** *(the latter of celebrated memory) crosses the ruins of* **Haucourt and Malancourt villages,** and ends at **Montfaucon.**

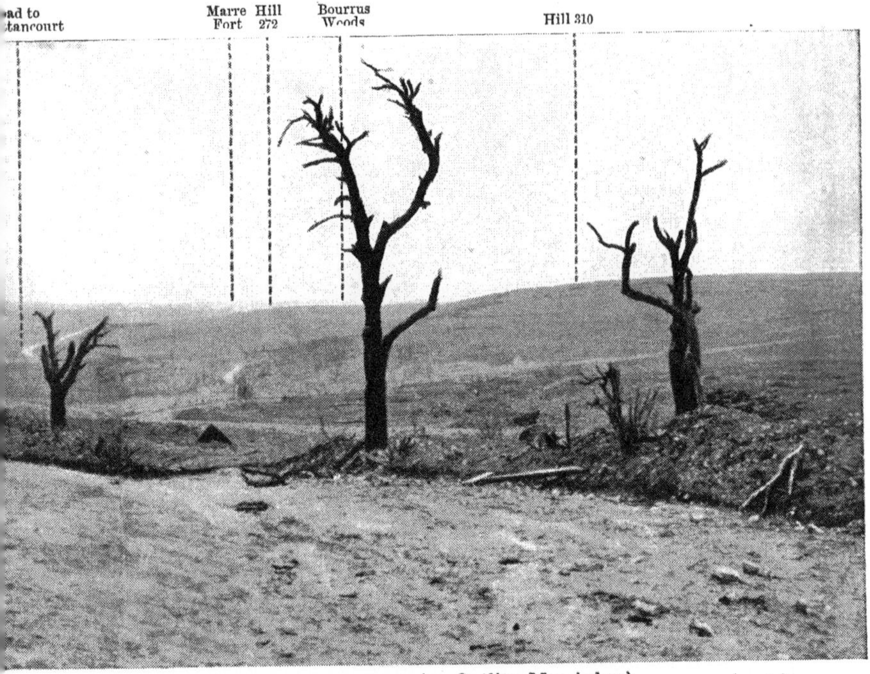

ad to
tancourt
Marre Fort
Hill 272
Bourrus Woods
Hill 310

TAKEN FROM THE WAYSIDE CROSS AT ESNES (*see* Outline-Map below).

MEUSE
Marre
Ft de Marre
Cumières
Ft de Bois Bourrus
B. de Forges
Forges
Chattancourt
Bois Bourrus
295
le Mort-Homme
272
de
Béthincourt
Ruisseau
310
Esnes
Panorama
N
Eglise
Chateau
Calvaire d'Esnes

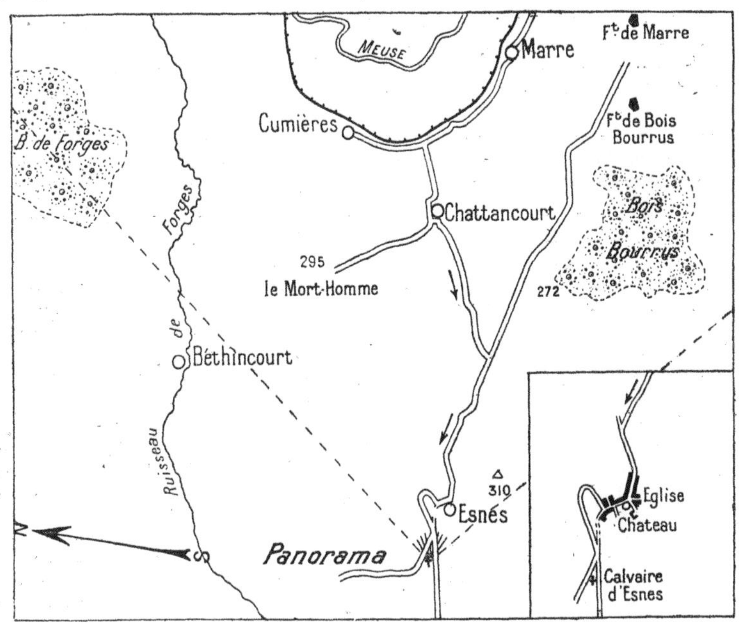

OUTLINE-MAP OF THE GROUND COVERED BY THE ABOVE PANORAMIC VIEW.

THE TOP OF HILL 304, SEEN FROM POMMERIEUX PLATEAU.

HILL 304

Hill 304, with Hills 287, 310 and 275, forms from Malancourt to Marre Fort a line of natural fortresses, which kept under their cross-fire not only the roads of approach, but also the bare glacis and the abrupt escarpments immediately bordering them.

The covered ground nearest Hill 304 is the S.E. corner of Avocourt Wood. It was from this wood that the IInd Bavarian D.I. left to attack the Hill on March 20th, 1916.

They were checked, however, on the long barren slope leading to the ridge, by the French cross-fire. Their three regiments, on March 20th to 22nd, lost from fifty to sixty per cent. of their effective strength, without gain. On April 9th, before Hill 287, the first German attacking wave succeeded in crossing the French first-line trench, practically destroyed by bombardment. They were running towards the French supporting trench when the survivors of the front-line trench, coming out of their shelters in the upheaved ground among the dead, exterminated them to the last man.

On May 3rd, eighty German batteries concentrated their fire on Hill 304 and its approaches. Clouds of black, green and yellow smoke rose from the hill-top as from a volcano, obscuring the sky to a height of 2,500 feet, according to the reports of aviators. As a British war correspondent put it: "The sky was like a dome of invisible rails on which fast trains ran madly." On May 4th and 5th a fresh German division attempted to occupy the position, believing it and its defenders to have been annihilated. They gained a footing on the N. slopes of the hill, but were driven back during the night by the French 68th R.I., which then withdrew. On the 5th the same German division attacked on the left the Camard Wood and Hill 287. In this wood, entirely levelled by an eleven-hour bombardment, the 66th Line R.I. first held up, then charged the assailants at the point of the bayonet At Hill 287 a battalion of the 32nd Line R.I. likewise brilliantly repulsed two attacks. On May 7th, after a tremendous shelling, the enemy attacked Hill 304 simultaneously from three sides with troops from five different divisions. It was their greatest effort against this position. However, two French regiments of picked troops (125th and 114th), one company of which charged, to the strains of *La Marseillaise*, the Germans were thrown into disorder and driven back to the N. slopes. During the rest of the month the enemy counter-attacked

TRENCH ON HILL 304.

Reconquered August 24th, 1917.

continually, at times in force, as on May 18th, 20th and 22nd, but without success.

On June 29th and 30th they sought to turn the Hill from the E. and W. with the help of liquid fire. On the E. desperate fighting took place around a work which was lost by the French on the 29th, then retaken, lost again, and reconquered on the 30th.

The Germans made a powerful attack on December 6th, in which they took several trenches on the E. slopes.

On the 28th of the same month another German attack, preceded by an intense bombardment, failed.

In 1917 the enemy continued their efforts against Hill 304. They succeeded on January 25th in occupying several of the French advance-positions, which were partly recaptured the next day.

Further enemy attacks on March 18th, 20th and 29th were repulsed after hand-to-hand fighting.

On June 28th and 29th another powerful enemy attack succeeded, with heavy loss, in capturing Hill 304 and advancing between the Hill and the S.E. corner of Avocourt Wood, to a slight hollow known as the **Col-de-Pommerieux.** This hollow was, however, reconquered on July 17th by the French 51st and 87th R.I., supported by two battalions of the 97th D.I. (335th and 346th Regiments), and one battalion of the 73rd D.I. After a remarkable artillery preparation, the French infantrymen, in half-an-hour, reached the fortified crest, and regained a kilometer of ground, including the famous "Demi-Lune" Redoubt. The 87th R.I., composed of men from the north, Valenciennes, St.-Quentin and Lens, went 300 yards beyond the assigned objective and captured an observation-post in front of the crest, which they christened "*Le créneau des Gretchen.*" The attack occurred at the time the enemy troops were being relieved, 520 prisoners, belonging to at least three different divisions, being taken. From a single sap the French Grenadiers brought out four German officers, one of whom, on descending the hill, turned back to admire the manœuvre of the French soldiers.

On August 24th Hill 304, the approaches to which had been reconquered on the 20th, was carried by the 139th and 121st R.I. (26th D.I.). This division, which attacked before Hill 304, on the Pommerieux Plateau and at Camard Wood, captured prisoners belonging to five different German divisions. After capturing Hill 304, Equerre Wood and Souvin Redoubt, the division attacked again on the evening of the same day, this time carrying the positions of Palavas, Alsace, Gateau-de-Miel and Lorraine, and advancing the first French line to the Forges stream, *i.e.* more than two kilometers from its starting-point between Haucourt and Malancourt, the latter still being occupied by the enemy.

On leaving Hill 304, *descend to* **Haucourt** *and* **Malancourt.**

Haucourt hamlet, on the Fontaine-des-Aulnes stream, was attacked by the Germans on April 4th, 1916, and taken after several sanguinary setbacks

MALANCOURT.

General view seen from the ruins of the Church in May, 1919.

on the night of the 5th after a fine defence by three companies of the 79th R.I., which held their ground against a brigade. It was recaptured on September 26th, 1918, by the First American Army.

Malancourt village was re-occupied by the French on October 13th, 1914. Enemy attacks on the following 16th and 20th failed. From February, 1915, the French lines were advanced to the slopes on the N. of the village. In 1916 the Germans did not attack until the end of March. They were unable to enter it on the 28th, but the next day captured two houses. On the night of the 30th they occupied it entirely.

Malancourt and its wood were recaptured by the First American Army on September 26th, 1918. The wood was hard to take, as the Germans had installed numerous blockhouses and barbed-wire entanglements.

GERMAN OBSERVATION-POST IN THE RUINS OF MONTFAUCON CHURCH.

Montfaucon

From Malancourt tourists may go to Montfaucon, three miles away, by a rather difficult road which has been summarily repaired.

From Montfaucon, where the Germans had established an observation-post in the ruins of the church, there is a complete view of the whole of the battlefield north-west of Verdun, from the hills on the right bank of the Meuse, to Vauquois.

See Panorama and Map on pp. 106 *and* 107

The tower of the church, which made a fine observation-post for the Germans, was destroyed by the French artillery. When, after their brilliant offensive of September 26th, 1918 (*see p.* 24), the Americans drove the enemy from Montfaucon, they found this observation-post (*photo below*) built with materials taken from the ruins of the church.

THE OPENING IN THE OBSERVATION-POST, THROUGH WHICH THE PANORAMIC VIEW ON PP. 106 AND 107 WAS TAKEN.

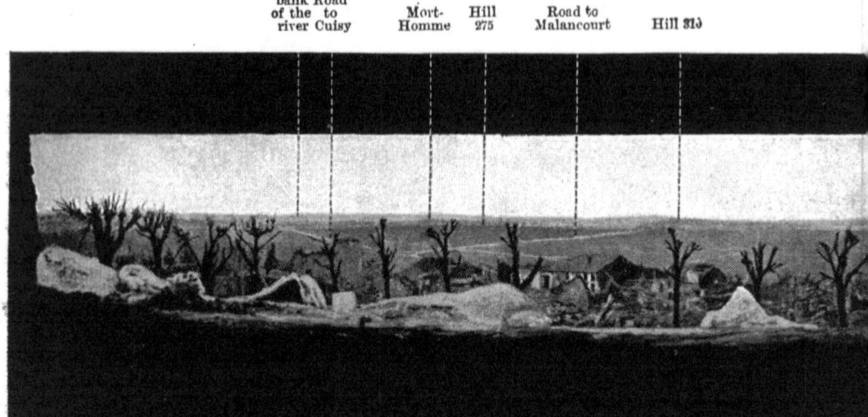

PANORAMA OF THE BATTLEFIELD O

The above view was taken from the inside of the Observation-Post seen in the photo below, the camera looking through the slit-like embrasure.

GERMAN OBSERVATION-POST, *through the embrasure of which the above Panoramic View was taken.*

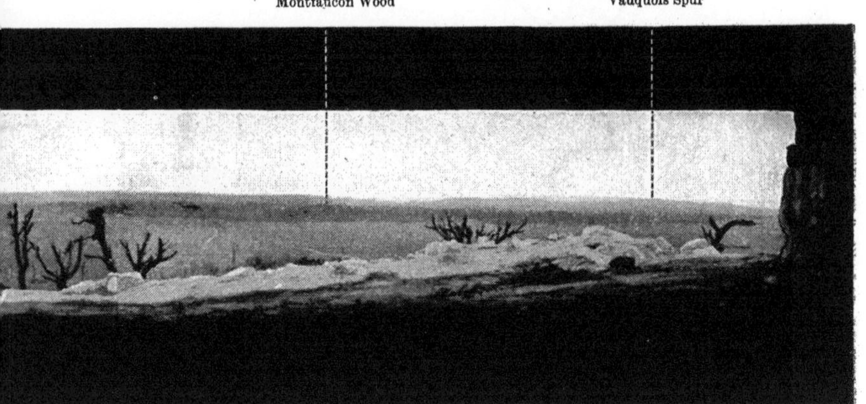

VERDUN, SEEN FROM MONTFAUCON.

In the foreground are vestiges of shell-torn trees and the ruins of Montfaucon Village. Verdun is on the horizon between Mort-Homme and Hill 275.

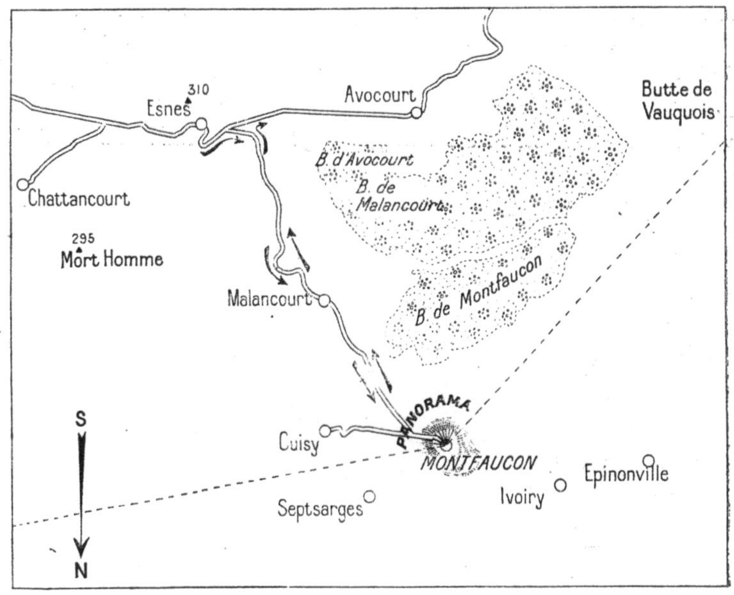

SKETCH-MAP OF THE BATTLEFIELD, AS SEEN BY THE GERMANS FROM THE EMINENCE OF MONTFAUCON.

AVOCOURT VILLAGE IN MARCH, 1916.

VI.—From Montfaucon to Avocourt

From Montfaucon return by the same road to Malancourt.

The bad state of the Malancourt—Avocourt road (*May,* 1919) *does not allow it to be taken from the former to the latter locality.* (The road passes through the woods of the same names, disputed with incredible fierceness.) *The tourist should, therefore, return to the Wayside Cross at Esnes, along the same road that he came by.*

From Esnes Cross (*see p.* 100), *take on the right the road to Avocourt, which marks approximately the extreme limit of the battlefield W. of Verdun.*

Avocourt and Avocourt and Malancourt Woods.—One of the finest feats of arms in the Battle of Verdun was performed at Avocourt.

On March 20th, 1916, the Germans, who had never been able to take the village, attacked with a fresh division of picked troops (IInd Bavarians), which had taken part in the summer campaign in Galicia and Poland with

THE CROSS IN THE MIDDLE OF AVOCOURT VILLAGE IN APRIL, 1916.

TRENCH IN THE RUINS OF AVOCOURT VILLAGE IN APRIL, 1917.

Mackensen's forces. The attack succeeded, with the help of liquid fire. A French counter-attack on the 29th by the 210th R.I., and a battalion of the 157th, recaptured the wood and the redoubt known as the "Réduit d'Avocourt," situated on its S. edge. The attacking troops, which had not been revictualled for four days, had finished their reserve rations twelve hours previously. So fatigued were they that they slept standing despite the bombardment. To rouse them, their chiefs, at 3 a.m. next morning, ordered the buglers and drummers to play. As the day was breaking the music suddenly stopped, a shell having buried all save one drummer. Furious

SITE OF AVOCOURT VILLAGE IN NOVEMBER, 1918.

MALANCOURT WOOD IN 1916, *seen from the French lines. The sand-bags mark the German lines.*

at this, the men, with the drummer at their head, rushed forward, and by 8 a.m. the wood had been entirely reconquered.

In 1917, hard fighting continued in this region with varying fortune. Powerful German attacks gave the enemy a little ground between Avocourt and Hill 304, and in Avocourt Wood. On August 20th, the French 25th D.I. drove the enemy from the S. part of the wood, advancing 1,200 yards and capturing 750 prisoners, thirty machine guns and ten trench mortars.

On September 26th, 1918, the wood was entirely cleared of the enemy by the First American Army.

Malancourt Wood.—It was against a French trench in this wood that on February 26th, 1915, the Germans made use of **liquid fire for the first time,** special pumps, operated by pioneers of the Guard, being employed.

VII.—Avocourt to Aubréville

From Avocourt take the road which follows the small valley running southwards (see Itinerary, pp. 88 and 89). It was on this road, hidden from the view of the enemy, that the French concentrations were carried out in the rear lines.

Two kilometers from Avocourt, take on the left the road leading to Hesse Wood, scene of all sorts of concentrations, posts of commandment, dressing stations, batteries of artillery, depots, etc

This road is in good condition almost as far as Aubréville, with the exception of two or three places on leaving Hesse Wood, beyond Bertrame's Farm.

VIII.—From Aubréville to Verdun

On entering Aubréville, take on the left N. 46 *which skirts the St. Menehould—Verdun railway.*

The tourist passes through Parois and Récicourt, where numerous cantonments and rest camps were installed for the relief of the troops.

Dombasle, where a large munitions depot blew up, is next reached.

From Dombasle one of two Itineraries may be chosen to return to Verdun.

The first, by continuing to follow the National Road, via Blercourt.

The second, which follows the crests dominating N. 3 *from Paris to Metz.*

For the second Itinerary, on leaving Dombasle, take the small road on the left, which leads to Sivry-la-Perche, 4 *kilometers distant.*

N. of the latter village, at the N.E. extremity of Hill 357, there still exists an observation-post, from which there is a general view of the entire rear-ground of the battlefield W. of Verdun.

If it is desired to visit this observation-post before the descent leading to Sivry-la-Perche, take the Béthelainville road on the left for about 700 yards, going thence on foot to the right in a N.E. direction. The observation post is about half-a mile further on.

From Sivry-la-Perche continue along the road, which passes first on the left of **Sartelles Fort** and then to the left of **Chaume Fort.** These two forts only played a minor rôle in the battle of Verdun, and suffered but slightly from the bombardments. In front of Chaume Fort there was an observation post for heavy artillery, whence there is a splendid view of the Meuse Valley.

From Chaume Fort the road is rather steep and in bad condition. Going down on the left and flanking a hill is Glorieux Cemetery, near the evacuation hospital.

Verdun is entered by the Porte-de-France.

IN THE RUINS OF VERDUN.

CONTENTS

REFUGEES FROM VERDUN DISTRICT PASSING THROUGH SOUILLY ALONG THE "SACRED WAY."

www.ingramcontent.com/pod-product-compliance
Ingram Content Group UK Ltd.
Pitfield, Milton Keynes, MK11 3LW, UK
UKHW041846190726
13854UKWH00002B/738